Thomas F. Hargis

A Patriot's Strategy

Thomas F. Hargis
A Patriot's Strategy
ISBN/EAN: 9783337042073

Printed in Europe, USA, Canada, Australia, Japan

Cover: Foto ©ninafisch / pixelio.de

More available books at **www.hansebooks.com**

A PATRIOT'S STRATEGY.

BY

THOMAS F. HARGIS.

LOUISVILLE, KY.:
CHAS. T. DEARING.
1895.

DEDICATION.

To those who favor a more perfect Union, the establishment of justice, the inculcation of pure patriotism in every American heart, this book is dedicated.

A PATRIOT'S STRATEGY.

CHAPTER I.

THE village of Roan is located in a valley of natural beauty and is the county site of Branch County, Kentucky. There the bluegrass grows in odd places, but westward, becoming thicker, the fields, matted with it, are one unbroken blue. Waving wheat and tall hemp are interspersed with blue pastures, kindled by the sun and dotted over with shades of sugar trees, black walnut, cherry, the ash and the oak. Under these, in the sunny seasons, blooded cattle and southdowns ruminate, or thoroughbred dams and colts seek shelter from noonday heat. These fields and pastures roll in every direction over low, undulating hills, which are broken by cool brakes and rest upon ledges of limestone. Here the rich red cheeks and very white foreheads of finely-formed men; women with chestnut brown hair, deep chested and perfectly modeled, strong and graceful, are to be found in exceptional uniformity, without a like elsewhere, in Europe or America. The valleys of Branch County lie level with the surface of her sister counties to the westward, but her moun-

tains tower in blue lines above and far away to the
eastward of the Bluegrass region. The waters, fed
by cascade and mountain torrent, flow gently at Roan
and the fells that environ this little village are the
foot hills of the cloud-capped Cumberlands. Lock
Ege's rock, around which eagles wheel, forces its
bald head toward the sky as a storm signal to the
Southwest.

On a sultry July evening in 1861, the muttering
thunder boded a storm. Lock Ege's rock was in
mist. Black clouds suddenly appeared in the open
sky above the western horizon and hung heavily over
the village. Soon the rain in misty waves was falling, like gray curtains, before the mountain tops,
which seemed to rise behind them and thence into
the hooded clouds about Lock Ege's bald head.

Oliver Hazzard Perry Patter, by Kentucky custom
and courtesy a "Colonel," who, with a Colonel's air
and pride and a Colonel's voice, had publicly read
the Great Declaration on the last glorious Fourth
and delivered what was afterward called, by way of
eminence, the "Eagle Oration," dashed, at break-
neck speed, under the roaring storm, into Roan. He
was mounted on his piebald stallion, Long-Leaper,
named in honor of Michigan's future Chief Justice
and the chiefest pensioner among ten thousand of the
War of Politics.

At each bound of the noble brute, the "Colonel"
shouted, louder than the increasing thunder peals,
"Bull Run! Bull Run! Hurrah for Beauregard!
Hurrah for Jeff Davis!!" At every leap, his ulula-

tions grew fiercer and his big, black, felt hat swung wildly around his revolutionary head, on which the heavy rain drops were falling.

He flung himself from Long-Leaper's back, threw the reins over the hitching-post and sought the barroom. There he burst upon three patriots, who were winding up an excited talk about secession, and deprecatingly shouted, "Gentlemen! My countrymen! Why are you idle here? Is life so dear or peace so sweet as to be purchased at the price of chains and slavery? Your country is in a blaze of war! The Patriot Army is marching upon the Capitol! Hark! The thunder rolls, the lightning flashes! Bull Run is bloody with the slain! The battlefield is yet dark from the cannon's smoke—yes, darker than the black clouds above us! Its gloom was rent with flashes from the red artillery, brighter and deadlier than the lurid lightning which now makes our nerves to quiver and us to dodge from each new-born bolt! Awake! Arise! or be forever fallen!!" He imitated the voice of the actor in this patriotic and Satanic appeal to arms.

The horripilation of Tom McShite's hair increased the alarm of his companions, but, when he arose to his feet, and in quavering tones shouted, "Hurray fur Jeff!" Eph Soaks cried, "O do, for my sake, stop!" Fate Wolf, though mentally dishonest and morally opaque, understanding the little motives of life and the little possessors of big motives quite as well as a pensioner understands, in the light of the Act of '90, the moral cowardice of a nation's dema-

gogues; and, being endowed with credulous cunning
and some capacity, though antecedent generations of
ineffectual education had beclouded his mental forces
and confused his mother tongue, saw at once that
Tom McShite and Eph Soaks were about to be
alarmed out of their loyalty and said, much after the
spirit of the Missouri Compromise, "I'm fur this
hyur New-Tralty, at the present, but I haint nothin'
now ag'in Jeff Davis, nur I never had much, ez bein'
he wur a Mexiken soldier en ole Ruff en Ready's son-
in-law." Giving Tom McShite a knowing wink, he
added, "En Jeff mout take Roan ef people went to
flouncin' thur tongues tu much."

"Did not I," said "Colonel" Patter, moved by the
predictive, orthodoxical spirit, "say in my last oration, called by some .'The Eagle Oration,' that calamity would befall this Nation falsely so called, that
the words of the great Declaration 'all men are created equal' did not include negroes, because of their
woolly heads, thick lips and pungent graveolence;
but that the charges against George the Third, closing with the ever memorable words, 'he has excited
domestic insurrection amongst us,' pointed to the
abolitionists, who are criminally assaulting an institution, bottomed on the sacred examples of the Bible
and vouchsafed by our glorious Constitution?"

The patriots gave "Colonel" Patter a congratula-
tory shake of the hand and joined him in a drink at
the bar-counter, on which he laid off the battlefield
of Bull Run.

He explained the relative positions of the two

armies and particularly located Jackson, where he received the immortal sobriquet, "Stone-Wall," from the tongue of Bee, whose drooping hopes revived as the deathless compound of fame fell from his lips.

"Off here in the valley," said "Colonel" Patter, pointing to the locality in his improvised war-map, "is where Joe Johnson gave Patterson the slip, and, like Blucher, arrived on the field just in the nick o' time to save the day and rout the cowardly abolitionists."

Fate Wolf, becoming deeply impressed, remarked, "I've bean turrible strong, all along, fur this hyur New-Tralty that Garret Davis en Crittenden got up, en Lincoln said they mout try tel they wore it out, yit I've bean a leetle shaky on it more nur wunce, en right hyur I turns a new leaf, en ef I don't change, nur haint turned back by nuthin', I expects to jine Jeff Davis ef he takes en kin hold on to Kaintucky."

Tom McShite's hair was settling down while this adroit explanation was developing, and, his returning self breaking out, in approval, he shouted, "Them's my sentiments," and "Colonel" Patter repeated himself, touching the drinks.

Eph Soaks, who drank and listened in silence, had been booming around the little town all day, singing Union Dixey, a Northern song with a Southern tune, and, therefore, felt stronger in the Union faith than his compatriots, who were somewhat stampeded by "Colonel" Patter's martial manner of imparting the news of the disastrous battle. The latter had procured a Cincinnati Enquirer containing a description of the fight from the captain of a steamboat that descended the Ohio the day before and brought the paper thence, in hot haste, to Roan.

Then and there "Colonel" Patter proposed to raise a rebel regiment, but Tom McShite said, "I can't see good at night. I'd like mighty well to wait fur daylight, then I could see better about jinin' your company."

"Company," interrupted "Colonel" Patter, "I'll raise a regiment or nothing."

As Tom McShite refused to join until daylight, the other two refrained also, Fate Wolf saying, "I can't see powerful good at night nuther."

Verbal hostilities went on, however, with the flight of night, the Abolition army being the object of violent bombardment for its cowardice in flying from a handful of rebels, for its free negro proclivities and weak Generals.

At last these agitated men broke up their rouse and "Colonel" Patter sought the summer night's air to fan his fevered cheek while he rode homeward to put to sleep his ambitious dream.

"The third trial is the charm," said he, but this time the restless horse stooped with a low whinny and "Colonel" Patter triumphantly mounted and rapidly rode off into the gloom of night.

Eph Soaks, in the local idiom, "laid out," as the beasts of the field do, because he despised a closed room, in summer, and, also, wanted elbow room, if the enemy should come. Fate Wolf and Tom McShite considered closed doors the safest and took the same bed, which was located over the bar-room. It was of peculiar construction. Resilient slats were nailed to the posts, on each side, one foot above the surface of the couch. Any man, "sometimes drunk and seldom sober," who got into this paradoxical bed, though his mind was made up to leave it early, found his body in the morning determined to keep it late.

This antithesis is after the style of Lacon.

Hardly time to breathe thrice had passed when Wolf and McShite fell into a quarrel over interpersonal accusations of disloyalty based on statements made by the Cincinnati Enquirer, whose editor was always telling the truth to help the rebels, or writing lies to keep out of prison. Twice a fight nearly ensued between them, but, as neither could get out of bed, they agreed to disagree for the night, and concluded to stand solidly by the Union in the morning if the rebels had lost the battle. A deep sleep soon fell upon them and hushed the clamors of self-preservation, which seemed at war with the demands of patriotism.

Early next morning Penn Grabbé, who had procured a secret contract with the Government to recruit, by persuasion, in Kentucky, appeared in Roan and immediately denied that the rebels had gained the battle of Bull Run. "Colonel" Patter soon showed his colors again, and, having hitched Long-Leaper, denounced Penn Grabbé as an Abolition spy, and at once threw open the bar-room to free drinks and for raw recruits. All day long, amidst the coming and going of the excited community, Penn Grabbé and "Colonel" Patter contended for the three patriots, but, as night hovered over the beautiful valley in which Roan reposed, Penn Grabbé drove off with Tom McShite lying in the bottom of the wagon, too weary to sit up and possessed of that devil—a divided opinion—alternately, but indistinctly, shouting, "Hurray fur Jeff!" "Up my Uncle Sam!" leaving "Colonel" Patter worrying with cunning Fate Wolf to convince him that a man ought not to want to live always.

"Colonel" Patter bought a Cincinnati Gazette at the same time he purchased the Enquirer from the steamboat captain, but carefully concealed that fact until Penn Grabbé had gone.

Now that the danger of production of a counter-Gazette had disappeared and Fate Wolf still hung fire, "Colonel" Patter's creative mind saw the opportunity to use the enemy's own sword against him and with it cut the Gordian knot. He hatched up a pretense and retired to a room in the log tavern to rest, but there his vigilance, like that in the motto about the price of liberty, preserved its eternal nature, and, in less time than it can be told, he cut from the Gazette its big name and pasted it over that of the Enquirer, at the top of the latter's first page, and returned to dispel Fate Wolf's illusions. He took him aside and confidentially showed him what the Gazette said about the battle. Fate Wolf was astonished! He read it over and over, and finally, fixing his eye on space, his left hand holding his right cheek and the counterfeit Gazette hanging loosely at his right side, slowly said, "Ez the great Gazzytee hez turned rebel, I mout ez well foller trumps;" but added, "howsumever, I hev my doubts whethersumever enny man hez a right to kill another fur a few niggers what belongs to somebody else."

"Colonel" Patter swept this last position with such a fiery charge of eloquence that further resistance or parley was useless, and Fate Wolf, in high disgust, agreed to join the rebel army for sixty days with the condition that he would serve thirty more if necessary to put down the Abolitionists.

Eph Soaks, having during the day loaded too heavy for effective action, sought the shades of the waterbirches that skirted the banks of Whirlinglog Creek, which brawled by the little town, and there, secure from war's alarms, slept away most of the previous night's excitement and some of the day's deep potations. The slanting rays of the sun as it sank low in the west found the exposed face of Eph Soaks and burnt him into life once more. He turned over and his foot struck a crooked dead limb, which flipped upon his leg. He thought it was a snake! Scrambling in terror to his feet he stumbled from bush to bush, finally gaining an upright position. Rubbing his eyes to acquire a better opening, he saw the red sun dropping out of sight behind big, luminous clouds which were slowly rising above the western hill-tops, whose crested trees seemed to move and form lines like tall grenadiers. A moment's gaze was enough; he snatched his hat and made a wabbling tear through the bushes shouting, "Yonder comes that d—— Bull Run crowd!" and disappeared in the wooded sides of the mountain.

II.

FOLLOWING the events of the last chapter, Fate Wolf and "Colonel" Patter were constantly seen together. During the remainder of the summer their conferences were long and secret. They spoke of public affairs in low tones. The people were also filled with vague apprehension. The battle of Bull Run and its results startled Kentucky and for two months hushed the wrangles of the tavern, the street and the stump. Public meetings and political barbecues were quietly conducted and were marked by conservative expression. The social fabric stood unbroken, but the people expected it to fall. They discussed the progress of the war with less bitterness than public speakers had debated issues of the presidential campaign, and with concealed fears watched the drill of the Home Guards, but openly admired the gallant horsemen of the State Guard, in whose ranks rode men who favored the South. Cautious expressions of passion and lull in public excitement were but the suspicious calm that presaged the gathering storm which was soon to sprinkle the blood of her sons upon the lintels of Kentucky's homes.

Late in September of '61, when the gorgeous colors of the woods were fading and the crickets in the corn chirruped to the coming night; while nature was vibrating with the sybillant song of death and the darkies sought the 'possum and the coon, "Colonel" Patter, mounted on Long-Leaper, and Fate Wolf, astride his black steed, Flat-Foot, armed with knife and rifle, departed for the military miscellany gathering at Prestonsburg. Side by side—Marshal Ney and Nick Machiavel—they rode into that old town.

Alighting in front of Freeze's Tavern, they were received with a courtesy, shall we say, due to their apparent rank and lofty purpose; no, but not wholly unlike the landlord's name.

The weather was chilly; the foliage of the forest was dead or in the sere and yellow leaf; vegetables were exhausted and bread had risen to starvation prices.

The old town was full of motley-dressed men. Ragged boys, as brave as Hugo's Gavroche, incessantly sang Dixie. A few companies of uniformed State Guards presented a soldierly appearance. The manners of men had dropped the gay forms of civil life and assumed the mystery and rage of civil war whose mad folly filled every heart. All minds were wild with the historic valors of rebellious patriotism. Nothing seemed worthy of study but the cunning of strategy and the shrewd quality of human destruction.

The next morning after their arrival, "Colonel" Patter rose and sallied forth among the "Revolutionists," as he constantly called them. He made many acquaintances and his descriptions of the situation caused not a few to hail, with delight, his and Fate Wolf's accession to the camp. For several days, he progressed finely in good impressions; but the constant use of hyperbole, his favorite figure in rhetoric, soon broke the spell with which he seemed to have bound the town. Wagging tongues began to guy him, at a distance. He saw that too much talk would not advance his ambition to command the gathering army, and, at once, assumed the mysterious attitude of a man, clothed with authority, bent upon some great design. He drew the cork of his secret and it leaked out that he was a Knight of the Golden Circle, was possessed of a commission from Richmond, and that he had come on an exceedingly delicate mission. Hearing of these mysterious claims, the Colonel in command ordered his immediate arrest as a spy.

"In the guard house! Oh my country! Has it come to this?" exclaimed "Colonel" Patter to Fate Wolf, as the latter came running from the Parade Grounds, "that I, who have borne the heat and burden of the day carrying Kentucky out of the Union, should be subjected to this outrage, this cabalistic effort to keep down my military preferment! Charles the Second had his Cabinet Cabal! George Washington had his Conway Cabal! and I may profit by ———"

"Be keerful," whispered Fate Wolf, "en don't give 'em a chance ag'in ye, ur ye mout be hung fur treezon. Ye see that thar word hez 'tree' in it en hez a 'z' in the middle uv it, that's jist like a man a hangin' on a tree, en ef they git to spellin' it over, en a lookin' at the trees, yander on the banks uv the Chattaroi, en then ef they wus to see a rope when ye wus abusin' 'em, they mout h'ist ye shoar."

"What are you whispering there so long for?" shouted the guard to Fate Wolf. "Get away, or I'll fork you up with my bayonet."

This quite broke "Colonel" Patter down. Seeing that it was unsafe to talk or whisper, he wept.

Having recovered himself a little, he said to the guard, in the most submissive tones, "May I ask Mr. Wolf a question in your hearing?"

The guard looked at him with pity and contemptuously said, "Yes, if it don't mean treason."

"Mr. Wolf, where is my horse?" inquired "Colonel" Patter.

"Well, he's yit down hyur at the Freezin' Tavern a eatin' the trof en a nibblin' a little Revolutin straw, ez ye would a called it, the fust days we got hyur."

"Yes," said the imprisoned "Colonel," "that is true; then everything was Revolution and Revolutionists to me but ——"

"Stop!" cried Fate Wolf, "don't git no deeper in nur ye air."

"I see! I see!" mournfully said "Colonel" Patter, "this war will be a failure unless more consideration is given men of prominence."

"If you say, another time, the war will be a failure, I'll knock a daylight hole through you," said a rough, rigid-looking soldier, who had come up and was talking with the guard.

Alarm spread itself over "Colonel" Patter's features, but, pretending not to have heard the remark, he moved to the back part of the guard house, showing more nervousness than he was aware of.

There was a window in that part of the building and "Colonel" Patter cried, "Raise the sash, I must have fresh air! This phthisic is awful!"

The soldier, who had threatened to shoot him, said, "The old spy just took the phthisic a purpose to draw attention from his treasonable talk."

"Colonel" Patter became silent and Fate Wolf went away to watch his chance. That night he communicated with the "Colonel" from the narrow alley upon which the window of the guard house opened. The next morning, daylight revealed an empty guard house, "Colonel" Patter and Fate Wolf were miles away, rapidly moving upon the road to Roan. The third relief of guards was rigidly examined by the Southern Colonel as to how the escape was effected. It was suggested by one that it was impossible for so large a man as "Colonel" Patter to crawl through the little window at the rear of the guard house. The Colonel said, "Never mind the window; it's a good thing the old gasconader is gone. He was really no spy and our supplies are too scarce to waste on noncombatants," and so dismissed the guards with his compliments, for he had secretly ordered one of them to allow the escape. But, like James the Second's flight from William of Orange, "Colonel" Patter's escape from the Revolutionists was a hair breadth reality to him.

On the way back to Roan, "Colonel" Patter and Fate Wolf, though depressed, discussed the war in all of its developed phases and conditions. Now and then, one of the horses would step on a dry stick and break it and the sharp noise would cause an involuntary jump of the animals. The riders, whirling their faces to the rear and seeing no pursuer, would nervously jerk the reins and tremblingly shout, "Whoa, you old fool, that's nothing to get scared at!"

For a mile or more after the flurry, the disagreeing patriots would trend to a common understanding on the "failure of the war." They agreed that it had been prematurely begun and that it was being unwisely conducted. Having gotten far enough away from the Revolutionists for neither horse nor rider to be alarmed by the rude sounds of snapping sticks or rustling leaves, Fate Wolf's mind began to operate in its own inimitable fashion.

He said slowly: "Less you en me make up some trooths about our trip to the rebel camp, so we kin stand afore the people farrer nur we did afore we went to this hyur rebelyon."

"Revolution, sir!" cried "Colonel" Patter, "not rebellion."

"Well, I allus tuck 'em to be the same whethersumever it wur revolutin ur rebellin. Yit less us make up some trooths fur our pertection."

"Colonel" Patter said, "Truth is not made up like lies. Truth makes itself up and lies make you make them up and give you all the trouble they can while you are at it. You had better let the truth alone, and, as for making up lies, that's awful dangerous in these ticklish times."

"But yit, ye don't onderstand me, ur I aint yit onderstood myself," said Fate Wolf.

"Well, rejoined "Colonel" Patter, "when a thing is understood, you can understand it."

Fate Wolf went into a brown study for several minutes. "Some men," he said, "talks wiser nur they thinks, en says things they don't onderstand, but, yit, a nuther feller kin onderstand 'em."

"That may be true," replied "Colonel" Patter, "but how to make up truths and tell no lies, while you are at it, is most too revolutionary for me."

Fate Wolf was silent and "Colonel" Patter proceeded, "If I had said nothing about the Knights of the Golden Circle and the Richmond Commission, we would not now be fugitives from justice, scampering through the woods and across public roads while one of us looks to the right and the other to the left. We have been talking face from face ever since daylight and my horse, dumb beast as he is, has been scared so often that I believe the vulgar quality of cowardice is creeping over me like a half-dead lizzard. Now, I wish to confide a secret to you."

"All right," said Fate Wolf, "I'll confisticate it."

"Then, sir, it is this," said "Colonel" Patter; "I would not go through such humiliation, anxiety and agony again to become the leader of the French Revolution! But how am I to get back home in honor? The Union men (I no longer have the right to call them 'Yankees') have taken possession of Branch

County and all other important points in Kentucky."

"Jess stop a minit," said Fate Wolf, "I kin fix it. I'll tell 'em I jess went along with ye to fotch ye back arter we seed the elephant. Everybody are beknown to my Union sentiments. Ye kin hide a week in the woods. Lemme go among 'em. Then we'll trot ye on Long-Leaper into Roan, ez a returned spy. Ye kin make a speech en tell 'em uv our narrer 'scape en danger durin' uv the dreadful days we wus a spyin' on the rebels."

"Colonel" Patter, without suggesting "Revolutionists" for "Rebels," according to his uniform custom, acquiesced, turned off to the right and was quickly in the heavy woods of Catamount Creek. Fate Wolf rode on to the town of Roan. On the way he stopped at "Colonel" Patter's farm and said to Mrs. Patter, "Send him pervisions en a leetle sperits en leave 'em on the deer-blind whur Beach Branch cums into Catamount Crick. Say nuthin' to nobody. Then cum back across the mount'in at Lock Ege's Rock."

The reader will note that while Fate Wolf is an irregular speller and neglects some of the rules of grammar, he finally drags his ideas in fair living condition from under the dead fall of confusion. If this apology is acccepted, no more will be made for him.

Penn Grabbé, who had recently returned from camp Dick Robinson, whither he had carried another load of recruits under his contract for live stock, met Fate Wolf at the Tavern in Roan.

Mutual recognition was quick, but the latter took

the start of Grabbé by shouting, as his sides shook with laughter and his big dirty-blue eyes filled with water, "Now jess hold on. Ha, ha, ha! Oh, ho, ho! Wait untell I'm dun laughin', ha, ha, ha! Whoo whee! This hyur war beats the wurld! I've had more fun en larned more about this hyur rebelyon than ever I knowed afore, ur expects to larn ag'in."

"Stop," cried Penn Grabbé, "I have recently heard that you once stole a free negro boy, by the name of Fate, and carried him off in the night, and that while being sold on the block as a slave, at Lexington, Jack May, now a rebel Colonel, who had pursued you in your kidnaping expedition, appeared, stopped the sale, had you arrested and took the poor boy home. I have also heard that the name you bear is a nickname applied to you from that act. If these facts be true, you can not fool me with your Rebel-Union loyalty, or explain your recent trip to Prestonsburg——"

"Thair now," interrupted Fate Wolf, "don't commit yerself no furder ag'in ez good a Union man ez ye air afore ye git the top en the bottom ez well ez both sides uv that thair story. Sum people say one side is good tell t'other is told."

"Then it is often better," interposed Grabbé, "so go on."

"But I say nary side is good tell the bottom en the top is put in, fur a tub wi' no bottom nur no top won't hold water, less more sperits, at the price you charged the Guverment fur Tom McShite's turnin' ag'in seasesshun."

The last hint put a stop to Penn Grabbé's little Spanish Inquisition and started him to thinking how Fate Wolf discovered the existence of the contract for "incidental expenses."

"I have collected no money from the Government for spirits," said Penn Grabbé, rather sulkily.

"Ef ye haint kerlected it, that don't show ye haint got it charged ag'in the Guverment. I seed the score, '63 qts.,' on the bar winder, en ye haint the man to stand to lose it, en the Guverment ——"

"Hold on," interrupted Penn Grabbé, in pliable tones and with a forgiving smile, the tendency of Fate Wolf's talk becoming too suggestive, "tell us about your trip."

"Didn't ye never hyur uv how the British captoored Fillydelfy? They tuck it, en it tuck them. That's the way me en 'Colonel' Patter cum out at Prestonsburg."

"Now that you have got 'Colonel' Patter back, what must we do with him?" remarked Penn Grabbé, converting Fate Wolf into an advisory friend of Government.

"How do ye know I've got him back?" asked Fate Wolf.

"Well, he was seen with you on the head of Catamount Creek yesterday morning."

"That's so, en jess leave him to me; I'll fotch him in en git him to make a injured speech ag'in the tirany uv the rebels en git him on our side yit."

"That is good! Excellent! Tell him the Government will give big bounties and pensions for all our

Union kin before this war is over, and we expect all the real business element of the State to join the Union army."

"That's wun uv Peck's idees," said Fate Wolf. "I've bean a sightin' along that gun baarl myself, en it'll do shootin' shoar."

Penn Grabbé laughed and asked, "Shall we meet to-morrow?"

"Y-e-s, s-i-r," responded Fate Wolf, "fur this hyur war beats ennything ever I seed, en we must keep up with the percession."

Next morning he reported that "Colonel" Patter had gone, but whither or for what cause he was unable to tell. "Onless," he said, "it wus on a spyful expedition, which wus turrible dang'rous ef he wus to be captoored ag'in."

III.

THE Grabbés, who subsequently had two letters added to their name, by patronymic changes so common in America, were of French extraction, but crossed with Puritan stock, long before the names of Wolf and Montcalm became jointly immortal on the heights of Abraham.

The Grabbés had left Canada anterior to the historic event last noted, and but little is, therefore, known of their antecedents. They settled on the Hackanum River, which flows into the Connecticut a short distance below Hartford. Selecting a romantic spot near its source, they quickly built a dwelling and began that home-like life which helped to fill the hive of humanity whence many swarms since their day have flown northwestward. Finally, by Search, Impressement and Insolence, the British broke the peace of thirty years, and the American Congress, inspired by a Kentuckian, declared war. In 1814, the Blue Light Convention met in Hartford, and, with closed doors, discussed subjects and methods which still rest in the mists of secrecy.

The Grabbés received lasting impressions of the impolicy of the war of 1812 from one of the delegates who lived on the Hackanum. He told them in plain terms that it was a democratic war inspired by Napoleon (whom, he knew, they detested); that it was carried on to popularize anti-federal politics, of which the country had had a sickening surfeit from the hands of that educated plebeian, Thomas Jefferson; that the war was impolitic because it jeopardized the trade and traffic of the New England States and set their commercial spirit back a century; and that all these evils were attempted to be justified on the ground that a few unidentified Americans had been seized for the needs of the navy of the Mother Country in her numerous wars against that national robber, Bonaparte.

These arguments, the ancestral loyalty to England, which unreasonably exists in Canada to-day, and an impending draft on the Hackanum, caused the Grabbés to leave behind the curving currents of the picturesque river, the wintry hills and the circling mountains of Tolland County, and to permanently settle in a new haven of rest in the wild country adjacent to the deep blue waters of Erie, whence Michigan and Ohio's dividing line runs due westward. In the new home a son was born who was destined to become the greatest strategist of the War of Politics. These pages are written to rescue his fame from oblivion and vitalize his virtues for the benefit of future generations of his caste.

He was born on the eighth of January, 1815, just as a flock of wild geese, storm sent, was flying like "a great arrow through the sky" toward the canebrakes of Kentucky and the rice fields of the South.

On that day Wellington's veterans were riddled by Tennessee and Kentucky rifle-balls and Packenham, the brother-in-law of the Iron Duke, was slain. All this occurred on the left bank of the Mississippi river, just below the city of New Orleans, after peace had been made.

Mrs. Grabbé, having heard of the great victory before christening her son, pondered on the augury of circling wings and war's red omen and inclined to name him Andrew Jackson, but his father preferred Packenham. The puritan mother knew too well how unpopular that name would be to let her son wear it, and, finally, to shield the child's future, persuaded her husband to throw aside military names altogether and adopt one of peaceful significance. Thus he became Penn Grabbé, partly in honor of quaker religion, partly as a tribute to the civil maxim, "The pen is mightier than the sword." After the custom of New England, he was educated in mathematics and mechanics. Through heredity and training, he was prudent and far-seeing. He never assumed responsibility of an undertaking before calculating the chances of success or failure. In cases, however, of high grade of doubt, he has been known, after calm consideration, to say to another, "You might as well try it, for mankind has some chance of success in anything."

Along the same meridian the wild geese had flown at his birth, he came to Kentucky, seeking richer fields of living, and settled in Branch County the same year the Know Nothings were so bad. Shortly after his arrival, he joined the nearest Know Nothing Lodge, and began teaching school. He soon disclosed an inclination to participate in public affairs and organized a Debating Club, in which he cultivated and displayed pure cunning of mind as distinguished from information or principle, and made it plain that a republic which clears the way to any office for all men will early produce the adroit and disputatious quality of the Greeks or the *vivida vis animi* of that one-languaged people.

But beneath the sea of words poured upon American soil from the shores of every stream lying between the Himalayas and the Guadalquivir or that flows into England's channel or the Baltic, lie hidden the rocks of confusion, equivocation and demagoguery. Many words becloud the energy of thought, cloak deception and mislead the ignorant. They are mightiest among the mighty forces against which truth and goodness contend. Hearts are hardened into stone by them. Souls, flimsy as white smoke, and consciences, weaker than a rotten thread, grow from wordy tongues, slow listeners and the passionate. In this land of great liberty, volubility is, often, taken for wisdom; passion, for eloquence; here the joke-teller retires the statesman; students of little motives, observant observers of local politics, fling their wordy commonplaces to the breeze of popular favor and stand with unblushing cheek and vapid thought in high places—but why specialize?—the mere and unspecified American verbalist—where is he not?

Penn Grabbé was not long in developing an ambition to serve the people in perquisitional stations. These manifested methods and tendencies were natural, for his ancestors possessed their evolutionary germs. The early Anglo-Saxon-Puritan created the protoplasm of profitable politics at the same time he was laboring to unify the double problem of civil liberty and religious slavery.

When a New Englander comes West to grow up with the country or to it, false modesty is left behind him; limits fixed to qualifications for office are cleared with one bound and, at once, he becomes a part of the community. Periods of probation disappear in the boldness or effrontery of his endeavor. The New England descendants of the West are the most adroit, persistent and successful politicians of the world's civil history. They can beat a hostile community out of its prejudices and secure its confidence while the native is drooping under one defeat or politically dying from another. After a public rubber of the best two out of three for an office, the voice of the losing native is silent upon the hustings, his dilapidated farm speaks poetically of the lost cause or his law-books are too dusty to handle, so he goes West or into desuetude, while, under like conditions, the New England emigrant thrives and finishes up with a victory.

IV.

ON the way to the recruiting camp with Tom Mc-Shite, Penn Grabbé sharked up a small list of "incidental" patriots. When he arrived, the Government owed him five hundred and twelve dollars, which was the contract price for thirteen recruits with incidental expenses. At once he made out a requisition for rations. It included spirits for twenty-six. The commanding Colonel asked, "Why so much whisky?" Penn Grabbé answered, "Because Kentucky patriotism must be kept inspired or it might become human and go with her Southern sisters. You can't tell what a man will do when he is opposing nature. He is just as apt to go back on himself as to go forward on the enemy."

The Colonel thought a moment. "Grabbé, you are wiser than the children of light. You can continue the spirits."

There were but three thousand unconditional Unionists in Kentucky when the war broke out and no man knew it better than Penn Grabbé, for he had been Sheriff of Branch County and served one term in the Legislature.

Possessing quick parts and being a subtile reader of the interested motives of men, by the time the war opened he understood local affairs, influences and passions which governed them better than any man in that county. A small, keen, but lulling, black eye, ruddy face and a home-made smile greeted every one whom he met in need of a smile. But he could meet the serious with gravity. His tongue never became an unruly member, except when indulging the annoying penchant of asking questions. His features were regular, his beard glossy, black and very fine. His well-knitted frame lacked the easy grace of a tall man and the free elegance of long limbs and tapering fingers. He stood upon short feet with high insteps. His hands were small, the fingers and thumbs were slightly stubby and tipped with short, square nails. His health was buoyant and his animal spirits glowed like the realms of ether, though passion never fought a battle with virtue on the field of his soul. Material success engrossed his powers and the methods of strategy possessed his being. Indirection gave him mental joy, while direct methods tested his self-possession too strongly. He studied strategy and played the game of life, excluding excitement and sentiment from every move, as one incorporated with mathematics and severed from the pathos of human existence. He was not cruel, but an indirect law-breaker, seeking the law's avoidance, when it crossed the path of his purpose, and avoiding its sequence when caught in its violation.

During the fall of 1861 and the ensuing winter, he had delivered forty-three wagon-loads of recruits, averaging ten each to the various recruiting stations in Kentucky. For recruits he was to receive twenty dollars per head and all direct and "incidental expenses." The four hundred and thirty recruits came to eight thousand six hundred dollars. The Quartermaster agreed to that claim and gave him a voucher for it. The expense account was next presented:

>"*First Item*—Forty-three wagons and teams thirty days at $6 per day......$7,740."

"My goodness!" exclaimed the Quartermaster, "isn't that item too high?"

"No, no," replied Penn Grabbé, "the item is low. I knocked off all pieces of days and left out the sacred Sabbath, because the Good Book says, 'Keep it holy,' yet the expenses of the wagons rolled on. Another thing, Major Paymento, the rebels owned all the wagons and horses, in the various sections where I recruited, and the women, invariably, fixed the charges against the Government at seven dollars and eight dollars per day, but I reduced the price to six dollars, agreeing to drive myself, in the event none of the recruits were sober enough to do so."

Major Paymento, at once, saw the difficulties with which the disloyal had obstructed the patriotic work of the indefatigable Grabbé and begged his pardon, saying, "Let this item pass, for this Southern woman's rebellion must be put down. They started it and are now put forward to obstruct us, because we can not arrest and shoot them as freely as we would their treasonable fathers, husbands and brothers, if they dared to charge seven dollars a day for wagons and teams not worth a cent over two dollars and fifty cents a day."

"Hold on," cried Penn Grabbé, "you have not heard the worst. They have put whisky up to four dollars a quart. Now, look at this item of incidental expenses, it will amaze you."

> "Item—Spirits for 430 recruits,
> 1 qt. per day for each recruit, 30 days,
> at $4 per qt............................$51,600."

"The Government won't stand that!" shouted Major Paymento, in a rage, jumping to his feet; "I know nothing of your 'incidental expenses!' Alexander the Great couldn't use up that much whisky!"

"Hold on!" said Penn Grabbé, "Alexander the Great, like General Grant, was a great lover of spirits! Mr. Lincoln himself has been hunting around for some of Grant's spirits to give to his other Generals; and I believe he would give $4 a quart rather than fail to get it; besides, here is my contract," handing it to Major Paymento.

After reading it the Major said violently, "This is a contract for cattle, horses and mules, and not for men."

"Hold on, you are mistaken," soothingly said Penn Grabbé, "it takes in all four species you have named. See, on the fourth page, just after 'cattle, 14 cts. per pound; mules, $200 per head,' the words, 'for recruits, $20 per head and all direct and *incidental* expenses.'"

"The officer who made the contract with you, sir,

ought to be cashiered," shouted Major Paymento, adding in the most dramatic way, "I have been in the regular army for forty years, and never heard of such a contract as this before."

"But, hold on," said Penn Grabbé, in kindly tones, "wait until you hear what I have gone through with on account of this item of 'incidental expenses.' A few days after the battle of Bull Run I got my first recruit at the town of Roan. There I met a rebel recruiting officer called 'Colonel' Patter, whom I had known in Branch County since the year 1855. That day's work was the hardest I ever did, and, while I got only one recruit, a soldier by the name of Tom McShite, who is still in the army doing good service as aid to a teamster, yet I so shaped public sentiment in Branch County that after all the rebels had volunteered and gone off and I *could* go back, I raised over a hundred equally as good as Tom McShite. But that first day's work cost the Government two hundred and fifty-two dollars for 'incidental expenses!' The rebel tavern-keeper had the score marked '63 qts.' on the shutter of the window. I can see in my mind's eye those figures to this day. They always remind me of that unfortunate Northern man, Rip Van Winkle, of New York. At another recruiting ground which I had picked bar-rooms were plenty, and I thought the 'Incidentals' would be limited, but quite the reverse, sir; quite the reverse! The tavern-keepers and tapsters were mostly rebels, and the few Union men engaged in these avocations had a false notion of the wealth of the Government and declared they had more right to charge four dollars per quart than rebels, and would take no less. The market was feverish from morning till night, as the supply began to fail to meet the demand. Finally blackberry wine and hard cider, dashed with spirits, went up to the high water mark. Then I was in their power! Without spirits they knew no business could be done by me for the Government, and they, also, were aware I did not intend everybody to go into the rebel army if I could prevent it. Sober patriotism is not aggressive in Kentucky, Major, and no Union recruiting officer can do much good in this State without spirits. I thought, at times, I would confiscate the rebel spirits, but soon saw that would be bad policy, as well as difficult to do. I got more recruits from their establishments, to which they induced Union men to come to convert them to treason, than from other places where none but loyal spirits were sold. I have heard the wives and daughters of rebel tavern-keepers say openly that Yankees should neither eat nor drink at their taverns, if they had their way. Many a time I have taken a recruit up to the counter to treat him after he had volunteered to become one of the noble band to save the life of the Nation, and there seen him insulted by the women, who would say, 'Eph,' or 'Tom,' or whatever his name might be, 'are you going into the Yankee army for a quart of whisky and sell yourself for thirteen dollars a month like an ox or a hired-out nigger?' The poor fellow's countenance would drop—my blood would boil—"

"That's enough, stop!" cried Major Paymento, "my blood is boiling, too! Let the 'Incidental' item pass! The life of this Nation shall be saved, if it breaks the Treasury."

"Major Paymento, I must thank you, not for the allowance of this 'Incidental' item, which will cost me more than it comes to in the long run, but for the quick perception and broad comprehension of the condition of loyalty in Kentucky, which you have manifested at each turn in the road of this conversation and settlement. Your surprise and indignation as we went along, before all the facts were stated, were as creditable to your heart as your present judgment is to your head."

They shook hands, the old Major looking bewildered and Grabbé feeling like Fouché after throwing his own police off the scent of a returned emigré, whose favor he wished if Napoleon should fall.

V.

"THINK of a State full of rebels treating the representative of the United States Government as Grabbé has been treated! He told me privately that his claims against the Government would scarcely pay him out of debt, and that in all probability he would be bankrupted by his efforts for the Union!"

A gentle knock on the door had failed to attract Major Paymento from his indignant and sympathetic thoughts. A repetition of the rap caused him to look around and cry, "Come in." The door opened and a young woman entered. Her open face was candid, and her movements very graceful. She had large, blue eyes, fair complexion, ligh-brown hair and a perfect forehead. Her chin, cut as if with a chisel, showed both tenderness and strength. She was in her twentieth year.

The Major arose and received her with the gallantry of an old army officer. He bade her take a seat and said kindly, "My dear, what may I do for you?"

"Nothing, except to get me the position of field hospital nurse in the army of the Tennessee or Ohio."

"There is no trouble to do that," said he, "but you are so young I fear the exposure might be too much for you."

"O never fear! for I am very healthy and my heart is in the cause. That makes one either brave, industrious or capable of using all one's power. It prevents weariness and gives to work zest and the attractiveness of well-doing."

"Hi, yi! You are a heroine and a philosopher, both in one."

"No, no! I am only in love with my country and humanity."

"What do you consider your country and humanity?"

Her eyes opened a little wider, the modest look grew stronger, and, with flushing cheeks and a sweet voice which shook slightly, she half exclaimed, "My country is America! My humanity, all Americans!"

"Your generalization would embrace the Southern Confederacy and the rebels!" was his quick remark.

"It was intended to do so."

Major Paymento thought deeply for a minute, then, turning his gray eyes full upon her, with a bright tear in each, said, "Child, you have started anew the lesson of charity which I was about to shut from my heart in my zeal for the Union. This *is* yet one country, and the rebels *a part* of humanity."

Just at this moment an aide-de-camp of General Bright entered in some trepidation and hurriedly stated that General Grant was being defeated at Pittsburg Landing; that all the available troops stationed in Kentucky were ordered to reinforce him.

The old Major never forgot his politeness in the presence of women, although he almost threatened to kill some of them during Penn Grabbé's recital. He had risen while the Aid was talking, and, when the latter finished, introduced him to the young woman, saying, "This is Lieutenant McCook. May I ask your name?"

"Yes," said she, "my name is Lema Sayr."

"Lieutenant, this young woman wants the position of field hospital nurse. Will you say to General Bright that I vouch for her?"

"I will," said Lieutenant McCook, and turning to her continued, laughingly, "It will give me great pleasure; but not so much as to become the hero of your rescue from danger."

She laughed pleasantly, saying: "How gallant your words are! You may have a chance to verify them, for I intend starting for Pittsburg Landing to-night."

"Oh, don't go! You might get killed, for fighting may go on there for a week."

"That will make it all the more important for me to be there to help care for the wounded," she said calmly.

Major Paymento looked upon her with great admiration and McCook appeared to be much interested in her fate. He extended his hand and with a gentle, manly bow said: "May I shake your hand as I say good-bye?"

She took his hand and with a brave look bade him good-bye.

Lieutenant McCook showed some lack of self-possession. But why should his spirit begin, without cause, to feel in need of consolation? Thinking thus, he departed, but he carried a new image with him, an image destined to rise in the vast war's dangers which were yet to close about him on an hundred fields.

Major Paymento invited Miss Sayr to go to his wife's quarters and await permission to act as nurse. Mrs. Paymento received her in kindly fashion and made her feel at home. She had not long to stay, however, for Lieutenant McCook returned in an hour with the permit and an unlimited pass to go and come at will. He delivered them and retired quickly and in silence.

A vague feeling came over her that his heart had gone out to her. What is it that intuitive woman does not know of the heart or its secrets, though they be seemingly past finding out? From the grasp of the hand, the glance of the eye, the tone of the voice, a bow, a movement, even from silence, its intangible currents are caught; noting faults, as she forgives them, and taking off the message whether the sender will or no. Love is always welcome to the heart of woman. If free from dross, even love that can never be enjoyed is a gracious thing in the heart of her heart.

At midnight the train started for the Tennessee. General Bright and staff were aboard. Lieutenant McCook attended to everything that night to make Lema safe or comfortable, yet he tried to keep his acts free from notice. The more, however, he strove, the plainer it appeared he was very attentive. At daylight, a steamer was taken on the Tennessee and Pittsburg Landing was reached before dark.

The great battle was over; the reverses of the first day had been cancelled by the successes of the second. The weary were resting and the wounded were dying. Decked with her cross of mercy, Lema was on the awful field just as the gloom of night began to gather in about the twenty thousand human beings who lay dead, dying and mangled on the damp ground, or scattered bleeding among the trees and the bushes, along the little rivulets, in the furrows of the old fields, on the plankless floors of cabins and hospital tents, which stood ghost-like in the dusk. She was sent, on foot, a half mile away, to Shiloh Church, which was full of the wounded of both sides. The soles of her shoes were wet with blood, and the hem of her dress was reddened, as she entered and beheld a sickening sight. It was her first experience. She grew sick, her nerves seemed about to give way and her fortitude ready to desert. A little camphor to the nose, a brave rally, and, seizing bandages and lint, she, heroically, joined the heavy-bearded doctors, who were amputating and binding in a most business-like way.

She labored and sorrowed all night, but, when the violets of light opened in the east, the long lashes rested upon her cheeks and the weary eyes were closed.

VI.

LEMA SAYR was of good old New England stock. On the paternal side, lawyers, statesmen and soldiers graced her ancestral line back to the emergence of Massachusetts from the barbaric darkness of North America. The maternal kindred gave scholars to learning, divines to the pulpit and virtue to the hearthstone. The writer dares not descend into many particulars of a life too sacred to permit the revelation of its sad facts and starved aspirations to the curiosity of a critical world or to open its pathos to the tenderness of the good reader's heart. Her pure heart had lost its first ideal, but she had borne her calamity with the grace of the triumphant brave. She had early learned the deep truths and inexplicable misery of first love. Thence her sympathy, wise, deep and tender, went forth, making itself a part of the disappointments of others. Often the wreck of her ideal, prone in the dust, had lain before her eyes and fain she would have lifted the diamond that still glittered even there, but, alas! she could only pity, she was powerless to save. Too proud to wear the willow, she lifted up her head, and, smiling upon the dejection of her own heart, began to plant roses in the fields of human trouble. She pushed the past behind her and faced the future. With white feet, she trode its winding way, and, with clean hands, ministered to the distressed.

The first sacrifices of the work of her hands were to her mother, left penniless by the premature death of her father. The cruel change of fortune scarred her pride; the alternate follies of the first man whom she trusted and who appeared perfect in her sight had rudely disturbed the sweet confidence of life which lives in the morning of every human existence. Her soul was early starved like an innocent lamb in parched pastures. But the wisdom of unhappiness was hers. The tenderness of misery was ever present in her heart. Joy, of which she was deprived, was transferred to others. She knew that the power of joy belonged to her; that though she could not fill her own soul with it, she could shower its blessings upon another. A spirit can be deprived of joy, but not of the power of giving joy! If it be more blessed to give than to receive, we know why the unhappy can create the qualities of heaven itself.

Later in life, while studying, by these lights, the life of another, she fancied that she saw pearls of great price in the depths of its stormy sea. Unwittingly she sought to raise these pearls by words, they were of faith and sympathy, possibly of admiration, but, instead, she stirred its deepest depths with an uncontrollable gale of passion. Brimming full, that passion flooded its shores and drowned his happiness. Sadly she weighed her deed, as she weighed all other things, and, by sacrifice, her favorite means to attain the ends of life, tried to restore the virtue she thought he had lost, but, in her well-meant effort, broke his heart to fragments. She believed the ruin wrought by her was for good and complacently gazed upon it until her mind saw its terrible mistake and then remorse overwhelmed her sensitive nature. Seeking to right the wrong she had committed, her heart became enthralled and a double misery seemed to weigh her down. He, whom she strove to assist, languished as other beings bereft of joy had languished and two lives alternately starved and flourished upon this new adversity. She sorrowed over the loss of his happiness as bitterly as Rachael wept for her children that were not and pondered of the burden she had added to his life. Thenceforward, she thought of the existence of sin; of how to lift up the fallen; of the strength of the wicked; of the weakness of the weak, and prayed for the betterment of all conditions. Her heart trembled with the candor of childhood at the possibility of losing a friend, yet a masculine purpose dominated her mind. She was a woman, however, whose bosom held a woman's faithful heart. She consecrated it to trouble and cultivated its indestructible power of conferring happiness upon others, while the masculine tendency of her mind pointed them to duty or suggested the triumphs of ambition. She had studied the humanities more wisely than she knew. By toil, sacrifice and economy she had made the New England home comfortable, freed it from debt and chased the spectre of want from its doors. Then the great, rude war, with its deluge of blood, broke upon her country, and, as a dream in the night, she disappeared from the quaint old gables, the maple-lined walks, from hearth and home, leaving behind, like a ship in the sea, no trace of the way she had chosen to sail "o'er life's solemn main."

She sought the field of war, the couch of suffering, the forlorn and shipwrecked, indeed. The first sight of the field of Shiloh made her turn pale and repeat, with deep pathos, the lines of poor, heart-sore Robbie Burns: "Man's inhumanity to man makes countless thousands mourn." The hideous spectacle, the red bandage, the knife, the needle, the saw, the bloody earth, stood in gory reality before her feverish mind as she slept and dreamt amongst the bloody cots of Shiloh's little church. Next night, exhausted, she had fallen into a restless sleep. Suddenly the deep groans of a wounded Confederate, who was being placed under the surgeon's knife, sounded in her ear, and, half awake, she sprang to her feet and cried, "Don't cut off my arms," just at the moment he was murmuring, "Don't cut off my arms," and the chloroform was subduing his senses. It was half delirium, half reality. She saw his open face, gray uniform, and was at his side. Stretching out her hand to touch him, as if to make sure it were all reality, it fell upon a rent in the sleeve of the gray coat that hung from the cot. She raised the bloody shreds into which the bullets had torn it and looked at them feelingly; she looked at his yellow-red hair and thought of the picture of Cortez in the rotunda of the Republic's Capitol.

His forehead was white and the struggling circulation which sent fitful flushes to his cheeks made it look whiter. The lips were apart and dry, the outer skin parched, but the carnationed flesh could be seen beneath. The breath was short and quick. The liquid black eyes were glazed. The shadow of death seemed to be creeping over him. The cheeks were pinched by suffering. The lacerated arm and its long, shapely fingers, with no blood in them, lay still upon the couch. A bullet had rent the muscles of the upper right arm and torn through the muscles of the back, breaking a rib in its wicked passage. The left hand was fearfully mangled by a minnie ball. The doctors were painfully adjusting those brave arms, resistless and senseless now, for the cruel knife. Lema Sayr's mind whirled, circling brain and thought.

She was upon her knees beside the cot! begging the doctors not to main so splendid a being. She said: "He is too young to be made a cripple of forever. I will nurse him to life and health. I know I can do it!"

The doctors, looking curiously at each other, walked off into a corner of the little church and talked together. They said something, but, what, no one knew. She thought it was about humanity, they looked so serious and so kind. They came back and probed his wounds.

"No bones, save one of the index finger and a fractured rib, are injured," said one.

She looked into their faces. The probing was done, the splintered rib was freed from its fragments and the arm and hand skillfully dressed and bandaged. It was over! and the doctors said, "Let her take charge of him," and they went on with their work, taking the chloroform but leaving restoratives.

Thursday morning he was feeling better. The shock passing away, he began to take notice of the persons who seemed so seriously busy in the little church.

At last his soft dark eyes ceased to wander over the results of Shiloh's tragedy, whose agonies were epitomized in that little church. Fixing his weak and weary gaze upon her face, he struggled to speak. His words seemed to flow and murmur. To catch his articulations, she bent low and caught the words, "Who are you?" spoken in feeble tones which reminded one of the touch of deftest fingers on muffled instruments.

"Who am I?" she repeated, softly.

"Yes," he whispered almost with a gasp.

"Only a nurse assigned to wait upon you until you are well," was the reply filled with tenderness like unto love's preparatory mood.

These words faintly softened his features, for his gratitude was touched, and that manly courtesy, which marks the bearing of Southern men, quietly made its appearance in his wan, smooth face. He was trying to speak, when she looked deep into his eyes and laid her shapely fingers upon her lips; he saw the hand and lower arm as the loose sleeve slipped toward the elbow and Joel Hart's genius, which made marble speak, crossed his dimmed recollection, but, before nature and art could coin words into thanks or compliments, she was gone to fetch the rich red wine to strengthen his weak struggles to be better. She made him drink of it and forbade him to talk. He could not understand quite clearly all she was doing or why she was there.

Reader, if you never had a minnie ball tear through your muscles and splinter your bones it will be hard for you to analyze the hazy mind, the benumbed feelings and clouded condition of this wounded Confederate.

Closing his eyes upon the weird aspect of things and people around, he saw mental pictures, which the heart helps to make as long as it can beat, of sweet home scenes, in the midst of which stood his sisters speaking to him, laughing, flushing all with smiles, amiability and tenderness. He saw the face of his anxious old mother. At a distance, among the sugar trees, standing deep in the bluegrass, he saw his father with upturned face looking into the branches where the bursting melody of a mocking bird's almost human song flooded the odor-laden air. Quail whistled from the hedge fence and black plowmen clucked to lazy mules in the sunny furrow.

Under the sweet influences of illusion's creations which the mind, for the priceless purpose of happiness, can enjoy until overthrown, and from the exhilirating effects of Lema Sayr's wine he fell asleep and slept for an hour; then quick, nervous jerks, as if catching at something to keep from falling, disturbed his sleep, and the piteous moans which he made told of the struggle within and of the work of cruel wounds. This wounded heroic man in uneasy slumber increased the current of sympathy flowing in her heart. As he slept she watched each painful line tracing itself upon his face until she suffered torture unspeakable. Now the drawn features would smooth out their wretched wrinkles, and then the pale face would break up its rigidness. The light of the April sun streaming through the window from the west, blending its golden hues with his white cheeks and bright hair and disclosing the strong lines of suffering in other faces, filled the little church with awe and mystery and laid bare the progress of the grim reaper.

The blessings of quiet seemed to slip into his face between the ridged lines of pain and contracted muscles. She studied the varying features and watched for the returns of exorbitant pain to collect its terrible tribute and write its broken and its curved lines upon the face of the sufferer. Her agonized heart abated its beats when she saw them coming. At intervals, when the wrinkles and writhing lines disappeared, she went to other cots and did many things for the wounded dressed in blue. She spoke to them words which were as good as deeds. Her ear was alert to the slightest sound from the cot of the gray Confederate, and often she hurried back to him with trepidation, tenderness and fear accentuating every look and movement, until assured that the restlessness was the assertion of returning strength, which began to manifest itself more and more as the precious hours flew by.

For several days he grew stronger, and, as the reaction became more potent, began to look at her frequently, and sometimes intently.

One day, about a week after the battle, he looked at her so wistfully that she felt she was bound to speak to him and test his condition. His liquid black eyes seemed to be brighter, or, rather, not so dull, and, though forbidden to speak or exert himself, his look spoke, and she concluded that a quiet conversation might be for his betterment.

"What makes you look at me so hard? Do you know where you are, or what has happened?"

He flared up and struggled to rise, but fell back and asked, with some vigor, "Did General Johnston win the battle?"

"No, he lost it and was killed."

A terrible exclamation escaped his lips, and the effort exhausted the little rally he had made. Great lines of torture crossed his brow and heavy gloom settled on his face. She was greatly excited and very unhappy at the result. She gave him a sedative and a little wine and water to strengthen. The exhaustion, the sedative and the wine invited sleep, and it came, as it so often comes, the only friend to misery and misfortune. With the hideous picture of his dead chieftain before his mind's eye, he dropped into an uneasy, but strong-breathing sleep. He cried out more than once, "Charge and avenge—"

She knew what he meant, and pity akin to love filled her heart.

VII.

THE first May morning of the dreadful year '62 opened upon full-blown flowers smiling on the graves of the fallen; upon woods, deep, shadowy and restless, which whispered to the breeze; and shone brightly upon the blood-stained floor of Shiloh's church and its white cots, from which had risen, convalescent, gallant forms dressed in blue or clad in gray.

"Miss Sayr," said her wounded rebel, as she had once called him, "I do wish you would go walking with me this sweet May morning."

"Do you think you are strong enough to walk?"

"Oh, yes," said he.

After carefully descending the steps of the church, they looked about a little before deciding which way to go. They concluded to go toward the "Hornet's Nest," so named from the hot resistance at that point made by the Union troops to the headlong assaults of the Confederate Legions. Coming to the place where McClernand made his bold stand to keep the Union Army from being driven and wedged into the angle formed by Snake Creek and the Tennessee they sat down on a moss-covered trunk to rest.

To their left were the overflowed bottoms of Owl

Creek, which is but another name for the upper part of Snake Creek. In their front heavy-leaved trees bent and nodded to each other, where Sherman made his final determined stand, thrusting his sharp salient into the woods through which the victorious Confederates, with faultless valor, were charging; while Ben Hur, vascillating around on the River Road, was beyond Snake Creek, jockeying for a good start as if beginning that chariot race which he afterwards won on paper. His doubt whether to go to Purdy, Pittsburg or Purgatory, dissipated his decision amidst the roar of the cannon and the shouting. Go to, Ben Hur! On the other side of the creek, where there were no rebels, you were dreaming of the Prince of India, perhaps of Indianians; but generous old Ulyssus forgave you, and so do the surviving Confederates, for a better reason.

All around them were long mounds of new earth stretching here under the trees, and there in open fields. Numerous graves heaved their solemn bosoms toward the pitying sky. Farther away, to their right and rear, the heavy woods whispered of Prentiss' surrender. The whole scene was pervaded by the highest and gloomiest tragedy of that bloody drama —Albert Sydney Johnston's death, just as his iron grasp was closing upon assured victory.

Occasionally Lema looked at her wounded companion to see how these scenes affected him. She had given him a little wine as a tonic, and it and the fresh air made him feel more buoyant than he had since he was wounded. She was afraid to talk to him of the details of the battle which had become as well known at Shiloh's Church as the overt sins of any of its members who may have furnished food for its dead gossips. She sought to keep his mind occupied and his feelings quiet. Birds flitted about, the flowers were gay, spring filtered into his being and fortitude and hope united to revive his spirits. Her eyes sadly surveyed the life in death around them. The old moss-grown trunk on which they sat, the moldering heaps of slain lying beneath the growing turf, the awful thought of the struggle which cost so many precious lives, crowded from her memory all else for the time. Even the dear memories of home were lost to mind, and her soul, bound with hoops of steel in unexpressed and inexpressible mystery to the destiny of her country, was there re-dedicated to its service. Yet from this sacred revery she snatched a sympathy for the wounded soldier who sat by her side, a stranger, a prisoner, and, in her estimation, a rebel.

They were each communing, in the same spirit, with the surroundings; each was enfolding the other in that all-embracing sympathy and distress of mind which cannot exist without a real personality to support it. Such conditions of mind and heart, sorrowing over the dead and the irreversible, reach out, as tender vines seeking the oak, and twine themselves about the living for support and life. The misery which springs from mental distress and finds sweet solace in its occult blendings with the feelings of a living, beating human heart, has never been fathomed nor described, and can never be, though human experience and philosophy were to unite and touch the dark secrets of the unknown.

"I have not been inquisitive, as Yankees usually are, else I would have known your name long ago," said she, withdrawing her eyes from the deep foliage that embowered the "Hornet's Nest," as if it were now a young bird's nest, and looking inquiringly into his languid face.

"My name is Robert Hope," said he, "if you *care* enough to know."

Blushing from the curves of the beautiful chin up to the very lashes of her blue eyes because he had laid stress on the word, care, Lema bowed her thanks for the favor of his name and nervously picked bunches of moss from the fallen tree trunk and threw them on the ground to which her eyes had fallen. Her heart fluttered like two little birds which were twittering and billing in a stately elm that shaded a long and mournful looking mound that lay a few paces to their right. She was taken unawares by his heavy and tender emphasis upon the word, care, and her hitherto dormant and unformed feelings flew to her cheeks before she could analyze them. Her self-possession seemed to have been assaulted by a hidden enemy and for just a moment all knowledge of self forsook her. She could not divine the volatility of her emotions until she thought of the overwork of the last three weeks and the constant strain on her nerves.

Summoning her fortitude, she made another effort

to know something of this brave man, enlisted in a bad cause, as she believed. But her voice quavered, in spite of her fixed purpose to be self-poised, as she said, "I believe I am feverish or nervous." Pausing a moment, she added, "I should like to know where your home is and something of the antecedents which must have influenced you to fight against your country. Tell me. It will be good to while away the time, as verbal autobiography is better than written, for the reason that you can afterwards omit the vanity without leaving the record behind."

"Before I comply with your request, madam, you will permit me to say that I am fighting *for* my country and there is nothing in my life which would justify vanity."

"Ah; well, never mind what I said about vanity; that was but a humor and we will not quarrel about what you consider your country, but agree that you are only trying to tear off one wing of the American Eagle."

"I wish I could wring his neck," said he petulantly.

She looked at him impatiently for an instant and burst into a subdued laugh at the poor fellow's peevish desire to wring off the head of the proud bird of liberty. She laughed until he began to smile and finally to laugh too.

In the midst of the humor which had taken the place of far different feelings, she said, "Don't wring the eagle's neck to-day, but tell me where your home is."

"It is in Kentucky, Woodford County."

"O yes," said she, "I've read something about it, and Bourbon County too, in Uncle Tom's Cabin."

"Yes, that monstrous exaggeration has some reference to it," was his reply.

"There it is again; wait until you get well enough and then I'll give you a peaceable quarrel over that book and the eagle too," softly said this loyal New England woman to whom he owed his life, for he had died without her vigilance, care and practical sense.

"I beg your pardon," said he, "for my rudeness. It was inexcusable, but I am not myself. Will you forgive me?"

"You have committed no intentional offense, I see, else you would not have asked pardon so quickly. It is granted, provided you will not demolish the eagle until you get well and are exchanged."

"Exchanged! I was thinking of escaping!" said he, as they arose to their feet.

Lema's face turned white, and, in a voice which was naturally persuasive, but trembling then with a new power, she said, "Would you escape now and let me return to the church suspected of aiding you? It would break my heart ——"

Interrupting her, he said, "I would die in prison before I would do such a thing; the thought dishonors me. I was thinking only of what all prisoners think and spoke from impulse."

"But you frightened me so much! by using the past tense in a present sense," replied she, "that I lost my self-possession, seeing that you had an opportunity, here in this thick woods, to escape."

He sought, by sly humor at her expense, to laugh away her suspicions and restore the confidential armistice which had existed all along between them.

"My position would be a very hard one in the event of your escape while in my charge."

"Oh, calm your unfounded suspicions; I would do nothing to compromise you, not even for the pleasure of wringing the eagle's neck," said he.

Then she laughed an indescribable laugh, one which touches the heart, and begged his pardon for misjudging his manhood.

They walked slowly back toward the little church but made a long detour to the left, tracing, in their route, an acute angle near the center of the Confederate right where Johnston fell and John C. Breckinridge led Kentucky's matchless Confederates in the final charge which broke the Union left into flying fragments.

O then for another hour of the Confederate chieftain's precious life! But new history, strange fames, a new map of America, would have been written; our country divided; the ills of frequent wars transmitted to our children and the date of Liberty's death anticipated by centuries.

As they gazed at the woods and the old fields, listened to the breezes in the branches, heard the songs of the birds flying about in the overhanging boughs and felt the power of the gentle circumstances of peace, a deep feeling of introspection took possession of their hearts, and, in silence, they threaded their way back to the church.

As with the lantern of Diogenes, Lema tried to search the bottom of her heart, but its gloom shut out the light from its depths and left her deeply doubting the capacity of any mortal to solve the problem, "Know thyself." She considered of her duty to her country and thought of nature's law which plants in every bosom hostility to spies, to informers and the treacherous, concluding she was not bound, by any principle of patriotism, to become an informer against Robert Hope and report the possibility of an attempt on his part to escape.

Next morning, the few wounded Confederates that remained at Shiloh's church were sent off to Paducah, thence to go north for confinement in prison as fast as their condition should allow. She had done something for every one placed in the little church, and, when each gallant Confederate bade her good-bye, each had a lump in his throat and a tear on his eyelashes, while his tongue said something about "Lema Sayr, the friend of humanity."

Robert Hope was the last to shake hands. A gentle pressure of the hand, a short, solicitous look, deep and tender, from one was returned by the eyes of the other—he was gone.

After their departure, she sat down by a window of the little church and placed her hands upon her heart for a little while as if she were pressing into manageable bulk the love of humanity which filled her bosom and weighed heavily upon her soul.

She arose very soon and sought the surgeon and asked if she could serve to advantage here any longer, and, if not, to be assigned a new field of labor.

"Well," said he, slyly, "we will send you to Nashville to wait upon Union soldiers alone, for these rebels are too courteous to ladies."

"Now, Doctor! I have only tried to be good to everybody."

The Doctor, seeing he was about to annoy her, soberly said, "That's so, and I will give you a good place, as good as we have."

VIII.

THE dawn awoke a deer-bird that had slept in the branches of a mighty beech which shaded the deer-blind. His first notes heralding the day broke the soft slumbers of a neighboring red-breast, which, opening its eyes upon the white lances of the new morning, poured forth sweet anthems to the day's nativity. A still more pretentious songster joined in with phrasing trills and flute-like strains that made the forest vibrant with tunes, the sweetest ever heard. Hundreds of feathered throats began to sing, and, before the light in the east had lanced the heavens to the meridian their leafy housing was filled with incessant melodies. The transcendant music flooded the woods and dark ravines with wondrous joy and floated into the ears of the dull and dreamy being lying motionless upon a mossy bank beneath. The gentle wind streamed through the branches of the trees and softly swept the wild flowers to the music of the birds.

"Colonel" Patter caught the deer-bird's primal warning of breaking day, and, as the swelling lays increased, steeping his senses with entrancing sounds, he reclosed his eyes and listened to nature's untaught musicians. And while eaves-dropping the wild birds he soliloquized of treasons, stratagems and spoils.

"My patriotism led me to the projecting precipice of alleged treason, from whose giddy heights ragged Revolution peeped through every rent in its unlooped garments with suspicious eye and marked my overwrought zeal for its victim. Its Robespierres incarcerated my body hitherto sanctified against the touch of violence. To escape their blind vengeance I outwitted the guard, fled the accursed place and betook myself to the wild but friendlier woods for protection. I have slept in lone cabins far up on the mountain side and hid in dark ravines, like a hunted beast, tortured by terrors and anxieties which drove courage from every extremity of my once proud corporate self. In chill November's surly blasts, through the falling dead leaves of the shivering forests, to avoid arrest at the hands of my wily companion, Fate Wolf, whom I could not then trust, I fled from this very spot over which now hover sweet songs and fragrance-breathing gales. In sequestered cabin, sheltering rock-house, relying at times upon the ravens for food, I passed the last long, cold winter, which froze the genial currents of revolution into the thin ichor of strategy, and now my soul is fortified for spoil! Here, in this enchanted place, I dedicate self to self and abandon the vile principle of destruction for the rich dogma of self-preservation."

He arose and, throwing his head back, while his countenance bore the image of simulated courage, hurled from his throat a shout of defiance that reverberated throughout the dark ravine. The birds ceased their songs. He mounted Long-Leaper and started to Roan for the purpose of surrendering to Penn Grabbé and trusting to his clemency and afterward acting with the non-combative ranks of strategy. With abated crest Long-Leaper, resembling Rosinante, bore his drooping master unheralded into Roan.

Penn Grabbé had received full particulars of the fearful tidings from Shiloh, and was feelingly relating the incidents of the battle to Fate Wolf.

"Stop!" shouted the latter, whose cunning and coarse humor never forsook him, "hyur cums 'Colonel' Patter, the eagle orator en the Owlsome spy. I know'd he'd drap in sumwhurs with news frum the rebel camps he's bean a follerin' all last fall en winter. Hit wur agreed atwixt us that he wus to play spy en help the Union all he mout fur the way the rebels entreated him."

"Hi, now, what news, Patter?" shouted Penn Grabbé, dropping at once to "Colonel" Patter's condition and significantly leaving off the hitherto proud fitting title.

"Grabbé, the miseries through which I have passed never forced me once to shed a tear, but, seeing that you strip me of my visionary title and drop into that familiarity which means contempt, I fear that you seek to vie with the revolutionists—I mean the rebels—to humiliate me and join your contempt to their suspicion and bloody designs which I narrowly escaped with my noble friend, Fate Wolf."

Penn Grabbé laughed immoderately at "Colonel" Patter's shrewd comparison of his own fall to that of

Cardinal Wolsey, and then, with great effect, addressed him as follows:

"'Colonel' Patter, Job says, 'Neither let me give flattering titles unto man,' therefore, I charge thee, fling away ambition. Love thyself first, cherish those hearts bent on spoil; adopt strategy, for it wins more than raw honesty."

"Prithee lead me in," said "Colonel" Patter, and they entered the tavern, and on the same bar counter he had laid off the battlefield of Bull Run he drew a moving diagram of evanescent rebel camps and said, "They are ragged, starving, sore-footed, scarce of arms, but mind you, gentlemen, as fightsome as wild tigers."

"That's adzackly so, fur it tallers with the Gazzytee en Enquircr when tuck together," said Fate Wolf.

"Colonel" Patter, seeing the moment was favorable, called for the drinks and proposed the following toast:

"With malice to nobody and amnesty for everybody."

"That's national logic on a peace basis," said Penn Grabbé, a touch of humor in his tone.

This was the sentiment Lincoln afterwards plagiarized for his second Inaugural address.

They drank the toast with hearty good will, and "Colonel" Patter was taken into full fellowship. The "Colonel" was requested by Penn Grabbé to go with Fate Wolf to deliver the next wagonload of recruits, and aid the latter, who was not much of a scholar, in settling with Major Paymento.

"If it will not be necessary to bear arms or wear a blue uniform I'm willing to accommodate you in this matter. But you know, Grabbé, how high-tempered the revolutionists—I mean the rebels—are, and that if I were caught by them with one of Garret Davis' Home Guard muskets in my hands or a Lincoln uniform on my back, they would fly into flinders and hold me to that Richmond commission, and might proceed to extremities."

"That will not be necessary. You can go along under the guise of a peaceable citizen working for the Government, but not fighting for it," said Penn Grabbé.

So entirely did these views relieve "Colonel" Patter's embarrassment that he broke out talking anew and spread his compliments us usual, closing his utterances as follows:

"You and Penn Grabbé, Fate Wolf, are natural born strategists, and destined to rise high in the service of the Government."

IX.

THE prisoners on the steamboat descending the Tennessee were carefully inspected. When Paducah was reached, many who had expected to be put off at that point were declared fit for prison and detained on board. They were uncertain of their destination; but when the steamer circled the northeast apex of land which projects into the mingling waters of the Tennessee and Ohio and began puffing against the current of the latter, they knew their doom—Camp Chase or Johnson's Island.

Robert Hope grew gloomy as his chances of escape diminished. The Falls of the Ohio were in sight; Louisville would soon be reached and passed; his spirits were drooping, for, once on Northern soil, he knew that a prison's privations, amidst the cold blasts of its winters, were almost beyond escape.

He feigned to be worse the night before, and, as the boat landed at the foot of Fourth street, his constant groans and pale face attracted the surgeon who had come aboard for the purpose of examining the sick and wounded.

The Doctor, at the first professional glance, was accustomed to give one of those off-handed opinions which genius prides itself in being able to give. The

A PATRIOT'S STRATEGY. 67

languid looks of Robert Hope appealed to him powerfully.

The first clerk of the steamer, who was at heart a Southerner, remarked, "This man has been in a bad way ever since we left Pittsburg Landing."

"Tut! Tut!" said the surgeon. "A doctor with a single organ of sight could by autopsy alone have discovered this man was suffering from marasmus. Send him on shore to Ninth and Broadway hospital."

"But, Doctor," said the sergeant in charge of the prisoners, "I have been with this man —"

"Go ahead with *this man*," interrupted the surgeon, "we have no time to listen to unprofessional opinions."

The Hoosier sergeant shrank back abashed at his own temerity and at once put Robert Hope on the wharfboat, whence he was carried to the hospital as the diagnostician had directed. The sergeant said to himself, as the boat swung from the landing, "Of all fools an educated fool is the most absurd."

The hospital was a long double brick of three stories, fronting on Broadway but breaking off in the middle to two stories which abutted upon an alley in the rear running from west to east. Robert Hope was placed upon a cot which might have been whiter, but for air and breeze it could not have been located better. It was in a small back room in the third story, and was placed near a window that opened upon the rear a few feet above the roof of the two story portion of the building. Thence one could see some distance northward on Ninth street.

At that season Louisville was, as it is now, picturesque and exceptionally beautiful, its surface reminding one of the ocean's unbroken bosom as it heaves, when the winds are still, to the ebbing and flowing of the undercurrent. The streets at right angles, unlike the cowpath crooks of Boston, are wide, straight and cool. They cut each other for miles under one view of the eye looking in any direction. The green-leafed maples, forest trees and shrubs of many different dyes skirt the avenues and grace the yards of commodious homes built on big plots of ground. Gardens, amidst wold of wood and flowers, are here and there cultivated. Travel over its area of twenty-four square miles wherever you may, and the eye, greeted by changing colors and gently broken beauties, is relieved of that stony aspect which chills the heart in great treeless cities; the ear is filled with the twitter or songs of birds which build their nests in the shrubbery of the yards and on the very trees of the streets. The murmuring falls, the great canal, deep, dangerous and useful, break the smooth river which fronts the city; and the wide champaign country, covered with herds and flocks, stretching away east and southward, adds its pastoral scenes to a situation inviting and historic. No later than the latter half of the last century the foot-fall of the Indian alone was heard in deep glade and shady forests where now flourishes the ornament of the once dark and bloody ground and the grace of the quadrilateral.

Southern women were admitted to the hospital to

wait upon Confederates who were thought to be very sick. They were allowed to furnish others with needles, thread and tobacco, but with nothing which might be converted into a bribe of doubtful guards. All doors of the first story were carefully guarded; windows were slatted on the outside with heavy pieces nailed to the frames, and pavement and alley adjoining the hospital were guarded at night.

The spirit of blood and persecution, coupled with the baser passion of speculation, was rampant. The lovely city, full to overflowing of western and border State soldiery, was intensely agitated and alarmed. The notorious "hog order" had not then been issued by Jerry Burr, nor the arrest of females ordered by "Boil" Bridges,—yet the grind of the iron heel was upon the neck of Kentucky, prostrate in the dust of indecision. Contempt for her people curled upon the lips of reckless soldiers, while renegades, old underlings and new faces, lined with envy and for the first time risen to importance, were snarling at the prosperous, the decent and the good, informing upon their neighbors, persecuting women, arresting old men and longing to crown confusion and corruption with confiscation. Danger attended the movements of every citizen, male and female, and charity and kindness to "rebels," well or wounded, stood for overt acts of treason.

Robert Hope had caught the current of events from fragments of conversation overheard in the hospital, and little Lexie Hallen, who was admitted to wait upon him, told him a good deal about the tyrant,

Bridges, nicknamed "Boil" because he was constantly in a rage. Instructions were issued by him to provost guards, a kind of bashi-bazouk, and to home guards, a sort of local bushwhacker, hitherto unknown in civilized warfare, directing them to arrest all ages, sexes and conditions; to extort false oaths; to bind in illegal bonds the peaceable, and, finally, to deter from duty civil officers on which the shaking remnants of social order depended. The "Instructions" gave "damages and compensation" against peaceable citizens for bridges burned and railroads destroyed by "Morgan and his men," whom "Boil" Bridges called guerrillas. They also forbade free elections and were afterwards supplemented by the erection of a prison for females, who were required to work for their oppressors from morning till noon, from noon till night. Their hands were too tender for the coarse needle of army clothes, and with bleeding fingers and drooping spirits they sank under the gross barbarity.

Robert Hope had told Lexie that he wanted to get away.

The child, then only in her sixteenth year, turned pale and trembled from head to foot.

The brave Confederate calmly talked to her until fear disappeared and the love of adventure, so attractive to the young, took its place.

That evening, in pursuance of the plan he had been maturing since his arrival at the hospital, Lexie rode out on the Shelby Pike several miles and carried a private note to an old Southerner who owned a large farm and fine thoroughbred horses. The next day Robert Hope appeared to be much worse and Lexie's aunts came to see him. While putting a fresh pillow under his head to make him more comfortable, a pistol was buckled on him. As they were leaving, Lexie, in low tones, told him that the new pillow had no feathers in it, but contained a full suit of citizen's clothes. That day her aunts went to see General "Boil" Bridges and asked for a permit to enter all the hospitals of the city, their purpose being to help the sick. Without suspecting their design, he said, "I am glad to see ladies willing to wait on Union soldiers," and promptly gave them the permit. Armed with that document of power and implied loyalty, they appeared at the hospital after dark. The doctors and guards were lounging about the front door, some talking, others smoking and several sleeping upon long benches. The permit was read by the guard at the Broadway entrance and they passed in without question. Ascending to the third story, they found Robert Hope pale and anxious. Just as they began talking over the details which Lexie had arranged, a guard entered and called for the permit. It was handed to him, and, after carefully reading it, he returned it in silence, retiring immediately.

What did this mean? Lexie's heart fluttered with excitement, and Miss Bina and Miss Julia lost some of that cool-blooded appearance manufactured for the occasion.

Aunt Bina said, "If old 'Boil' Bridges catches us, we are good for his woman's prison and the song of the Yankee Shirt for the rest of the war."

"Oh, what shall we do," cried Lexie.

"Be calm," said Robert Hope.

They stopped talking and listened if any one were at the door. All was quiet. No sounds were on the wooden stairway.

"Now is the time," said Robert Hope, and in a moment two window slats were loosened.

"Go quickly," said he, "and take position."

They were gone. At the east end of the alley leading from the rear of the hospital, Miss Bina and Lexie, with deeply anxious hearts, promenaded up and down Eighth street awaiting results. Miss Julia, being unable to stand further fatigue, went home. An hour had gone and nearly another, yet nothing could be seen in the alley, save the gleam of the bayonet in the moonlight at its western mouth.

A fire alarm was turned in on Ninth and Main. The unexpected sound frightened them so badly that they started to flee, but, like all other persons, they turned toward the fire and were possessed of a strong impulse to go to it. It attracted the guards because it had broken out in large government stores.

Robert Hope had, in the meantime, dressed himself as a citizen and swung to the top of the second story of the hospital. He was crouching and crawling over the noise-making tin roof toward the alley when the fire alarm burst upon the midnight air. He knew the power of a fire to attract attention even of the most sane and hurried his movements to the angle formed by the hospital and the next building at a point twenty feet from the alley. There he found the ladder which the faithful family servant boy, Ned, had placed in the angle. Covered by the shade of the crowded buildings, he quietly descended until half way down, when the frail stair broke under him and he fell heavily to the ground. Stunned and writhing in pain, he arose and hurriedly left the snaded angle and glided into the moonlit alley. To his left, rising over the first breakwater of the Falls, heavy columns of smoke filled the air. The glare of the fierce flames, mingling with the moonlight, the shouting of the firemen which rose above the whistle of the engines, absorbed the excited crowds gathering on Eighth and Ninth streets. He met a half dozen street gamin in the alley running as fast as their legs could carry them toward Ninth street. Cautiously emerging into Eighth, he faced, with indecision, toward the broad belt of light which the moon was pouring down upon Broadway and saw two blurred figures at the corner.

He approached and greeted them with, "a beautiful night, isn't it?"

They responded by taking him by each arm. He winced; gave a short, quick cry, "O, my wounded arm is broken," and they hurried along. In to Broadway, out to Fourth, and when Second was reached a body of cavalry, walking, trotting, laughing and singing, swung across the way and blocked their passage for ten minutes.

A soldier scurried from the ranks and, pressing his horse close to the pavement, asked, "Who are you, and why out so late?"

"We've been to a big fire at Ninth and Main and are going home, near Brook, south of Broadway," said Lexie as quick as a flash.

"O yes! We saw the light from the Highlands," and, satisfied, he spurred away.

Then Lexie and her aunt bade Robert Hope good-bye. They almost ran across Broadway, and, like phantoms, disappeared in the open black mouth of South Second street, where heavy trees shaded the junction of these beautiful avenues.

His escape had been discovered at the hospital and the provost guard were scattering in every direction, hoping to catch him before he could get into hiding.

Hearing horsemen coming behind him, he entered a yard full of heavy trees. Their shade hid him from view as the provost guards with clanking spurs and sabers passed close by.

Looking around one said to the other, "There would be a good place to dodge us."

"No," said the latter, "he would be afraid of dogs or of being taken for a burglar by the owner."

As soon as they had disappeared he entered the street again and wound his way through alleys, crossing large streets under the shade of the numerous trees, dropping into the weeds of vacant lots and hiding behind the projections from old walls as alarm or actual danger dictated. Weak from the pain of his broken arm and exhausted by exertion and anxiety, he was compelled, when the banks of the Beargrass were reached, to stop and rest. An abandoned wall, some of whose tumbled down rocks had rolled into the stream, ran close to its margin. He climbed over this broken wall and crawled between it and the water for a few yards. He could hear the hoof beats on the street leading to the Shelby Pike, and while prone on the ground a lighter tread in the open space between the wall and city smote his alert ear. The sound grew stronger, and gradually came in his direction. Then shuffling feet seemed to be slipping over the grass within a few yards of the wall. The noise of the steps appeared to stop at his very head; his heart beat violently, and cocking his pistol with great difficulty he awaited discovery.

"We certainly saw him go down the bank near here," said one of the human sleuth-hounds.

"It was lower down."

They moved farther away, and coming to the broken place where he had passed they got over and tipped across the stream on the rocks which had fallen into it from the dilapidated wall. He lay quite still until the sound of foot and voice was hushed, and then arose, half bent, and pursued his way in the shadow of the rocks in the old wall until he emerged into the open moonlight then streaming from the unclouded moon which had sunk far to the west. He took his bearings and bent his slow steps due eastward. An hour's steady walk brought him to the Shelby Pike, three hundred yards west of the tollgate, then kept by a rebel Irishman. On his right stretched a lawn in front of a white cottage.

While studying the situation, to his utter dismay two horsemen, with all the noisy equipments of cavalry, appeared in front of him. There was no time for deliberation. With drawn pistol he advanced, determined to shoot them from their horses. But no! He changes his mind; turns and lays down the cottage bars, except the top bar, steps through, leans upon the undrawn bar with "Lexie," as he called his pistol, between it and his bosom, and stands intrepid, clear-visioned and cool to receive the foe, making up his mind and steadying his nerve for the encounter.

They had seen him enter the cottage yard and heard his apparently careless hum of the "Star Spangled Banner," but thought it best to investigate so early a riser. Day dawn was beginning to fret the eastern sky, and they were in a hurry as bearers of dispatches to "Boil" Bridges, informing him of Morgan's approach on one of his wild raids. Turning their horses' heads from the pike, they rode up to the bars.

The Captain, as his shoulder-straps showed him to be, spoke and bluntly asked, "Where do you live?" emitting with his breath a good whiff of the scent of old peach, which Robert Hope plainly smelt.

Nodding his head backward he replied, "Up there in my little white cottage on the lawn."

"Where are you from?"

"I've lived here this many a day. But can't you tell me some news? Are the rebels doing devilment anywhere in the State?"

"O we can't tell," said the Captain; "flying rumors say that John Morgan is on a raid, but it may be one of the thousand false alarms the villain raises nearly every week."

Robert Hope had turned Yankee himself, and by asking questions soon blunted suspicion and caused them to draw rein and wish to be off. To be doubly sure, however, of leaving no doubt in their minds as to his citizenship, he boldly and kindly said, "Gentlemen, get down and take breakfast with us; we are early risers, it will soon be daylight and we always take breakfast at that hour."

The Yankees relaxed their bridle reins, the Captain cleared his throat and Robert Hope's forefinger touched the trigger of his pistol to be certain it was there. His suspense was intense. His heart flew about in his bosom like a weaver's shuttle and his knees became weak for an instant, but, seizing his nerve with his will, he began to draw his pistol.

The Captain said, "No," with a long drawl, "we can't stop with you, but would like to. We have dispatches, and delay, even of an hour, might be ruinous, for Morgan is coming and I must be going. Good-bye," and off they went.

Robert Hope reeled, caught his breath and exclaimed, "How near to death he was! What! Is this the hospitality of war! Invite a man to breakfast and shoot him if he accepts! This kind of hospitality was never taught in old Kentucky before. Uh! I am glad they didn't accept!"

He mused a moment, thinking that civil war was cruel, unnatural and rarely necessary. Before he could analyze the nature of the war or clearly contemplate its immediate effects or even darkly see its ultimate results, his mind reverted to his own predicament and in an instant he was moving, as a shadow, toward the toll gate. There stood the Irishman in the middle of the pike, just as Lexie had arranged it.

Robert Hope drew his pistol and advanced, but the rattle of wheels and the quick stroke of ironed hoofs upon the metal of the pike alarmed him and excited his overstrained nerves. He sprang to the top of a stone wall which paralleled the pike and tumbled over. Lying as still as his beating heart would permit and using the ground as a telephone, he heard the noise deflect from the road and stop in an orchard to the rear of the toll house.

He sprang to his feet, muttering to himself, "Lexie is a trump, she has won the trick again," and over the stone fence he clambered, scratching blood from his white hands and falling to his knees as he struck the earth.

"Up now and at the toll gate keeper!" said he, suiting action to words.

"Good evening."

"Gude avening."

"What's the news?"

"I undurshtand Margin's captoored."

"Well, that's all right."

"O, the latle gyrl has bane hure! an' it's yersilf."

Taking Robert Hope up bodily in his arms and setting him on the toll gatherer's platform, the Irishman called his good wife, who came quickly with an apron full of biscuits, chicken and "patates." She uttered many prayers for his escape and crossed herself at every word.

"The boogee is in the archid waithin' fur ye."
"Call it!"

It came whirling around the corner of the toll house and in half a minute Robert Hope was beside young Tom Mims driving for life and liberty. The next night a new guide was secured, and, mounted on the fleet horse furnished by the old Southerner, who was Tom's father, the vicinity of Frankfort was reached and sympathizers were again found.

There the noble animal was abandoned because it was impossible for a mounted soldier, even in disguise, to avoid the enemy, who were picketing and scouting on every road and by-path leading southward.

X.

"BOIL" BRIDGES had set a price upon the conduct of the best men in Kentucky. Like Rautenfeld, he had struck at the liberty of debate and election. He punished silence, stripped unarmed citizens of protection and sought to shackle thought itself in the secret chambers of the heart. Incapable of guarding the State against Confederate incursions, he vented his rage upon civilians and held them responsible for military acts of an enemy whom he could not control and dared not meet for fear of capture and the halter. This modern Cossack, without the Cossack's courage, this pretended soldier, half citizen, but thronging "in the troops of military men" as an enemy to peace, gloating over the miseries and misfortunes of his native State, miseries for which he had no sympathy and misfortunes he was incompetent to remedy, strove, as Satan would have striven in his place, to tear down the fabric of society that he might revel in chaos and confusion. He turned loose upon the pockets and peace of women and non-combatants the dastard spirits of domestic disturbance and bloody discord. Almost every cave, wood and hiding place in the unhappy State sheltered an embryo Confederate soldier. By appoint-

A PATRIOT'S STRATEGY.

ment, Robert Hope met Sunny Withers, an ardent youth of twenty, at Daniel Boone's monument, which overlooks the Kentucky river from Kentucky's cemetery, where "Glory guards with solemn round the bivouac of the dead." Clouds obscured the face of the moon, the wind shook the high tops of the cypress and the pine that now cast friendly shadows over the graves of brave young Horton and of the lamented boy Hunt, shot to death, while prisoners, without trial, contrary to all law, human and divine, by the black order of pretended retaliation signed by the gory hand of Jerry Burr. O that this blur could be erased from Kentucky's history by the recording angel! But it can not be done and the ignoble must stand in the dark background while the beautiful light of the brave, Union and Confederate, must illumine the picture of Kentucky's honor and fame. The night was alternately flecked with deep shadow and fleecy light as the clouds floated by, now obscuring, now incovering old Luna's solemn face. "Hold up your hand," said Robert Hope, yet he had never seen the face of Sunny Withers.

"You do solemnly swear you will faithfully perform the duties of a soldier of the army of the Confederate States for three years or during the war, and that you will support and defend the Confederate Constitution, so help you God!"

They shook hands and walked to Kentucky's Battle Monument, which raises its shielded head high above shadowed graves, above the tree tops and into the clouds, its marbled eagles gazing north and west upon the Capitol. On the eastern face of the monument the anaglyph of "Dick" Johnson killing Tecumseh stands out in bold relief, and the names of the sons of Kentucky, who fell for our country, are chiseled above the eagles on every face of the white pillar. They sat down upon the marble slab which covers the remains of young Henry Clay, who rests with the fallen of Buena Vista.

"Ah," said Robert Hope, "it fills my soul with solemn awe to sit like Marius among the dead glories of Kentucky and look upon her Capitol, where tyrants tread and speak and cruel proscriptions are hatched."

Young Sunny Withers drew a deep sigh, and, rising to his feet, exclaimed, " 'Boil' Bridges and Jerry Burr ought to have lived when Poland was dismembered! If the dead could rise, Kentucky would rise and drive these base sons from her sacred soil! Oh, let us go!"

With sad hearts, they left the sacred spot and sought the rugged hills and rough precipices of Glenn's Creek, and at day-break hid themselves in McDonald's old mill, which was idle because Glenn's Creek was low. At night-fall they sallied forth from the grim old mill, and, after an hour's quick walk, crossed the Versailles Pike. At midnight they reconnoitered the old homestead where Robert Hope was born. In the moonlight the shadows of the big sugar trees and great oaks, of the old elm and tall Columbian poplars, fell across and beyond the wide metaled highway which ran by Robert Hope's home, and, which, like a current covered with foam, rolled away over gentle slopes and wide depressions, between waving wheat fields and the blue bosoms of Woodford's swelling pastures. It was a long time till daylight. In yard and garden, on barn and mansion, over fields and woods, the moon shone down soft and still. Not a sound nor a disturbance broke the silence of the night. The two men crossed the stone wall that enclosed the wide grounds which surrounded this old Kentucky home. The deep bluegrass softly received their sinking feet. From the shadow of one of those old forest trees that stood so tall and silent, they crossed the moonlit spaces to another, until they reached the old cook's cabin which stood apart from "de white folkses house."

A gentle rap at the door.

"Who's dar?"

"Open and see; it's Robert."

" 'Taint no sich thing; Robert's killed at Shyloar."

"Oh, no, I wasn't; I am right here, Aunt Usley, but I am wounded."

This brought her to the door, and, when her old eyes fell upon the pale face of her young master, she burst into a flood of tears. .... In a few moments the clatter of cavalry was heard on the pike; the yards and grounds were full of bluecoats; every door of the mansion was instantly surrounded by a dozen or more dragoons, and loud demands of "Open the door!" were heard, but Aunt Usley's cabin was recognized as loyal by confidential inattention.

"Mos' Robert, you and yer fren git under Aunt

Usley's bade; dey won't cum in hyar. De Yankees sarched de white folkses house afore dis, but alys axed Aunt Usley to tell on de white folks, en she told 'em she would, but ye knows, Mos' Robert, she didn't," and, like many another Confederate, he trusted, with safety, his life and liberty to the old family servant.

God bless the old family servant! Though ignorant and in bonds, they were faithful to the ties of heart and to the love of humanity, which so often existed between master and slave. When the laborer and the heavily laden shall drop their burdens, the old family servant will hear the call of the Blessed Master, "Come unto me and I will give you rest."

Aunt Usley went out amongst the soldiers, but returned in a short time and said, "Mos' Robert, dey ar a'gwine to camp on ole Moster en sed de'r arfter you."

Robert and his comrade slipped out of the back door of the cabin into its shadow, and, keeping in the thickets of shrubs and rose bushes and shadows of the big trees, with the cabin between them and the guarded mansion, which was being rudely searched, they crouched away and were soon beyond the sound of sabers, spurs and speech.

Robert Hope's heart was sad, and the unseen faces of his mother and sisters, and his father's benevolent countenance and courtly manner, arose, as in his dreams among the bloody cots of Shiloh, to his mental vision and filled his heart with nostalgia's keenest pains. His disappointment grew to remorse, and, as he toiled on through the night, homeless and miserable. the horrors of war absorbed his thoughts; but finally its exactions dissipated his longing for home's sweet scenes.

XI.

YOUNG SUNNY WITHERS was of a cheerful spirit, smiled when he spoke and laughed at everything humorous; but, if tongues cut with a sharp edge, his spirit seemed to wince and sink at once to quietude.

Robert Hope became sincerely attached to him. Their communion made the night cheerful. They marched together around the most dangerous towns and military posts in the night and their toils became the labor of patient duty. The secret places of woods and rocks, which hid them by day, were solitudes of restful freedom.

They assumed the talk and put on the garb of cattle drivers returning from Cincinnati, whither stock could yet be freely taken, for the system of trade permits had not then been adopted, and thereafter they boldly traveled in daylight, continuing on foot along the public highways, like *ante-bellum* peddlers, with stick and bundle.

On the 18th of July they approached the northwest border of Branch county. At the junction of Blue Lick river and Whirling Log creek, on whose banks this story began, they hallooed for the boatman on the opposite shore, but Fate Wolf responded, "He's not hyur nur haint bean sense night afore last fur the rebels captoored him en tuck him off."

"Can't you bring over the boat?"

Fate Wolf was doubtful of the loyalty of the strangers, but finally, seeing no arms and knowing that "Colonel" Patter was near, concluded it was safe to ferry them over.

As they were coming up the bank to the point where Fate Wolf had hitched Flat-Foot to a pawpaw bush, "Colonel" Patter rode up on Long-Leaper.

"How are you, gentlemen? Cattle drivers?"

"Yes," answered Robert Hope, "we are just getting back from a hard trip to Cincinnati."

"What is the news there?" inquired "Colonel" Patter in his most sociable tones, to which Robert Hope replied, "Well, there is a good deal of talk about the rebels coming. It seems that scouts, spies and East Tennessee refugees report preparations and signs of a campaign in Kentucky by Bragg and Kirby Smith."

"That's powerful ugly," said Fate Wolf, "fur that geriller Morgan captoored Cythy-Ann yistiddy."

"What!" exclaimed Sunny Withers, but, to hide his mistake in unguardedly expressing evident interest, he laughed and wound up with the statement that "Boil" Bridges would have Morgan caught.

"That is very doubtful," said "Colonel" Patter, "for there was great excitement in Lexington on Tuesday when we delivered our last wagon-load of recruits to the Government. Some of the recruits wanted to come back with us and I expect lots of them left last night. Where do you live, gentlemen?"

Robert Hope, pretending to be very much alarmed, asked, in return, with great earnestness of tone and manner, "What would you advise us to do?"

Fate Wolf, ever on the lookout for recruits or surprises, interposed an answer between his mental King and Robert Hope's check.

"Jist go 'long with *us* en we'll take cere uv ye," winking at the boys as he said this.

"All right," responded Robert Hope, much more cheerfully than he felt.

Fearing that Morgan might come that way, they started for the wooded interior of Branch county and arrived after dark at the house of Penn Grabbé. Fate Wolf was the first to enter, and, winking at Grabbé, who welcomed him at the door as he passed in, whispered, "Think I've got two more recroots. Lemme manage 'em."

Grabbé shook hands all round and imitated a Kentucky welcome as well as skillful counterfeits represent genuine coin.

For three days the individuality of Robert Hope and Sunny Withers appeared to be swallowed up, as completely as Jonah, by the recruiting whale which had been engulfing all kinds of material since the battle of Bull Run.

XII.

THEY loitered around for a week or two, taking many trips about the neighborhood. At last Fate Wolf thought the strangers ripe for persuasion and jocularly remarked, "Bounties, boys! ef ye'll jine the army. Uncle Sam put in a Act last July givin' a hundred dollars to all boys who'll resk his life fur the old flag."

"But the 'resk' is the objection," said Robert Hope, "for what would it profit a man to save the old flag and lose his own life."

"The's hardly enny resk *a* tall in it fur we haint had *a* recroot killed yit," encouragingly responded Fate Wolf.

"Come, boys, just join for the fun of it, for big bounties, blue clothes, green money and future pensions," said Penn Grabbé by way of inducement.

"Well," remarked Sunny Withers, "it's very tempting, but we'd better wait a while and see how you get along."

"Of course we will not hurry you, boys; you can take your own time to think it over," kindly said Grabbé.

They broke off the conversation at this point to hear the news which "Colonel" Patter had received from a "Tiger Home Guard," who had just passed up from that famous horse-breeding region, the Bluegrass, with a better horse than the one he had passed down on a week before.

The "Tiger Home Guard" said that Kirby Smith was in the State and all troops and recruits had been ordered to Richmond to fight him, if he should come that far; this "Colonel" Patter plainly reported, without frills or hyperboles of speech.

The news created excitement, which soon abated because sober second thought discredited the bearer, who had cantered away on the pretty sorrel thoroughbred, whose small, leaf-like ears, long, shapely pasterns, high withers and lengthy limbs, clean and muscled as if wrapped with twisted thongs, would have made Rosalie Bonheur's brush speak another history of the horse's noble development in the New World.

Robert Hope was himself once more, barring the broken arm, which was not very painful.

Sunny Withers, yet a minor, was learning of war's conditions much of human nature which lies dormant in peace.

Fate Wolf's cunning was a patent ambiguity. Penn Grabbé's power lay deeper, and, to all the world, save himself, his strategy was a latent ambiguity which even the sharp probe of a Chancellor's conscience could not have reached.

Flying rumors daily swept over Branch county, whispering of the foe's advance.

Colonel Calfe had organized a regiment and established the system of extortion which culminated in Jerry Burr's "hog order" and the trade permits of "Boil" Bridges, as well as in the military robberies of General Paine, who made the people of Paducah pay him fifty cents for the privilege of drawing checks and ten cents for mailing letters.

In the fair county of Nicholas, where Colonel Calfe first drew the breath of life, he arrested the best and wealthiest citizens. For taking an extorted oath of allegiance or giving bond he charged large sums of money and viciously cursed the victims of his greed. His heart was black with envy, seared by conspiracies against his old neighbors and reeking with a half-civilized remorse for the cowardly murder of a poor, nervous inebriate, whom he shot to death under the forms of a pretended duel. The deed was done between the shores of two great States and by murmuring waters. The superstitious avoid the spot as they would the plague, and never speak of the murder without a shudder. Having filched by duress sixty thousand dollars from peaceful citizens and put the money in his pocket he marched for Big Hill.

On the way Penn Grabbé joined him with twenty recruits. Robert Hope and Sunny Withers, "Colonel" Patter and Fate Wolf rode among them.

"How did you mount your men?" inquired Colonel Calfe.

"The same way you made the rebels of Nicholas take the oath, give bond and pay the fiddler," replied Penn Grabbé, "by main strength and strategy."

Colonel Calfe expelled a dead laugh from his throat, his little, sharp, black eyes danced under his beetling brows and his long, hawk-billed nose touched the curl of his scornful upper lip, his lower lip completing a perfectly animal mouth.

"I'll muster in your men when we get to Richmond. Fall in behind my column and forage on the rebel houses. You can make no mistake. Every brick house contains a rebel. They have lived in luxury long enough, and I propose a divide! The time has come!"

On they went, depredating and roistering, until Richmond was reached. There was no time for delay. The enemy were advancing, and Colonel Calfe was ordered to proceed, without halting, to Big Hill. On its wooded sides he for the first time met soldiers of war. Being a fine shot and good woodsman himself, he ordered his freebooters to take trees, and they took them like frightened squirrels.

The Louisiana Confederate Cavalry moved to the onset. Their swords were out, the rebel yell pierced the summer air and the whirring shells crashed through the trees. Onward they came, like vengeance for evil deeds. The freebooters and their commander fled as sheep before the Beagles of New Zealand. Every road, by-path, field and wood was filled with hatless, scampering squads; "not a soul but felt the fever of the mad" and played tricks of flight more desperate than did the men of Manassas. Each man headed for the Ohio river, and made the fastest military time on record. General Nelson ordered the jailers of counties through which they passed to arrest and jail the cowards as deserters; but the jailers, not being as swift as the wind, caught none of them.

As they whirled in thick clouds of dust along Kentucky's broad, beautiful highways, many were the shouting inquiries made by citizens of this noble band who were fleeing for pay and patriotism. They gave no intelligent response until the hills and shades of Carlisle, where Calfe had put money in his pocket for oaths and bonds, were reached. Descending the slopes from the south, they passed a lawyer's residence whom Calfe had despoiled.

He shouted to them, "Tell me the news! Tell me the news! What's the news?"

No response greeted his anxious inquiry. At last, becoming desperate, he rushed to his gate and said to the hatless, coatless, unarmed horseman who was galloping in the rear, "D— you, were you whipped?"

"No," said this rapidly moving child of war, "we wusn't whupped, but wus moralized outen our places in the ranks en couldn't git back."

The noble band was soon out of sight, and the lawyer went back to his house murmuring to himself, "I knew a robber of unarmed citizens wouldn't fight. One night he threw a glass through a parlor window and cut the head of a lady to the skull, but he got knocked down for that. Now he's Colonel! What will become of this country?"

For months fragments of the freebooters were found all around the northern periphery of a circle more than one hundred and fifty miles from Big Hill, and reaching far into the war-like State of Ohio.

As the Louisiana Cavalry swept down the northern slopes of Big Hill, Robert Hope and Sunny Withers stood close to the trees which they had sought when the horse holders and Penn Grabbé's recruits had fled.

"Surrender," said a manly looking Confederate officer.

"With pleasure," shouted Sunny Withers. "Charge them! They are running like deer!"

"Give us guns!" cried Robert Hope, "we are escaped Confederates!"

But the cautious soldier said, "No, you had better be prisoners a while and then we'll see about who you are."

Placing them under guard, he pushed on in the chase. Soon the Louisiana horsemen were upon the rear of the flying fugitives, picking up prisoners and increasing the foe's consternation. After dark, when "the shout and din of battle" had passed Robert Hope and Sunny Withers were taken to headquarters. By their intelligent statements and candid bearing General Kirby Smith was convinced of their sincerity.

Next morning they were mounted upon horses captured from the flying forces of Col. Calfe and temporarily attached to the Louisiana Cavalry. The march upon Richmond was resumed, and Sunny Withers, bright and buoyant, laughed, sang and rejoiced in his youthful manhood. His beardless cheeks were carnation and his gentle brown eyes lighted a pure face. His black hair graced his youthful temples and his athletic young form, trained to the saddle, looked every inch a soldier. Gayly, cheerfully he rode by the side of calm, brave Robert Hope, whose quiet demeanor contrasted attractively with the gallant Kentucky boy whom he had enlisted among the tombs of Kentucky's sacred dead. They talked of their homes and hardships just passed and joyfully anticipated a quick return to the scenes of their childhood, from which one had so recently fled and the other been so rudely excluded. Aunt Usley's fidelity had to be rewarded, if they should ever see her again. The family reunion, parties and balls and gayety and the girls they left behind them were being discussed, when the boom of a cannon rolled over the hills and fields in front of them.

"The enemy are in front," passed from lip to lip.

The column halted for a few minutes. Men were dismounting, hurriedly tightening girths, adjusting accoutrements, remounting, turning about and nervously testing stirrup leathers by rising in their seats and thus placing the whole weight upon the stirrup. The rattle of musketry was heard. It grew louder and seemed to come nearer.

"Our men are falling back," said Robert Hope, and sure enough they were.

By the time it was dark, the enemy had advanced a mile or more and bivouacked for the night. From this position they were driven next morning in great confusion, but, being reinforced, rallied at ten o'clock and stood for another onset.

The brave Union General Manson, who had violated orders rather than flee, was encouragingly active. His brow bore the shadows of defeat, yet his unquailing spirit nerved his uneasy lines for the renewal of the fray as Cleburne's gray column, with the indomitable tread of victors, swung from the woods into Madison's brown pastures and waving fields of corn.

The steady gray line steadily advanced through shot and shell, closing the gaps of casualties by a right or left dress such as Southern infantry was wont to make on the field of glory when charging the double foe and attracting the world's wonders.

Churchill's Arkansians and Texans broke into a double-quick, and, with the inspiration of the wild, heart-chilling rebel yell, hurled themselves upon the right wing, while Cleburne's immortal infantry swept the left and center. Manson was still master of his own pluck. As if to fill his men with the mysteries of death and court its conveniences, he rallied his broken columns among the tombs and white shafts of Richmond's sacred necropolis. Here the last desperate stand was made. But the evil genius of defeat stalked through the grave-yard, and, while Manson's stout heart was breaking, his disordered legions broke and fled from the ghostly field, a panic-stricken rabble, seeking safety in unsoldierly flight.

The Louisiana Cavalry had gained the rear of the rolling, surging, demoralized mass. Manson, rising to the sublimity of genuine courage, drew his unfortunate sword. One hundred determined spirits, all that were left organized of ten thousand, followed it.

"Charge the road!" cried he, and it was cleared; but it filled again! Yet onward Manson rode, his little column dying at every step. The last scene of the bloody tragedy had come! The curtains of night were falling. The audience of stars came out upon the sky.

Manson, cool, desperate and admirable, rose in his stirrups and his gallant sword flashed in the twilight; a thousand Louisianans shouted surrender as their serried ranks advanced to finish the conflict.

Manson answered the demand with the order, "Advance and cut your way out!"

Concentrating his little band on a single point, he led it to destruction. Forty-two lay dead and dying around him. His noble steed fell under the brave rider and pinned him to the earth. Sunny Withers fell facing him. A pistol ball had pierced his lungs. The gray line swept by. His old mother, at that very moment, was thinking of his brave, bright face and recalling how it looked when he bade her good-bye for the Southern Army. Robert Hope was searching for him among the slain! Five thousand federal troops were sending up a deep hum of alarm and disappointment from the field while their surrender was taking place. Nelson, wounded, had escaped. Night confused all countenances and destroyed the power of recognition, except by touch and voice. The stars hung low in the heavens and calmly gazed down upon the exciting scene; upon the pale faces of the dead scattered over the battle's course for two leagues; upon the distorted features of the wounded writhing in agony; upon the plunging animals shot in harness; upon the wild horses, riderless, galloping over the fields, splashing into puddles of blood, and upon the convulsed features of the mangled remains of Sunny Withers.

Manson struggled from beneath his gallant steed and groped his way to the corse of the handsome youth whose last words he had heard. For a moment he looked through the gloom into the upturned face, it was too dark to see what else he did, and then sought his fallen army and surrendered with it.

The next morning a Confederate General and staff were passing, and, seeing a white handkerchief over the face of the dead, he dismounted. It was reverently removed, and the smile that had been worn in life still played around the pale lips, from which hung sprays of froth like white clematis. In the left breast pocket a New Testament was found, and on the fly leaf was this inscription:

"Remember thy Creator in the days of thy youth."

From his bosom was taken a small silken flag of red and white stripes delicately stitched together; stiff with blood and torn by the bullet which had slain his young life. In one corner of this miniature flag, skillfully worked by fair hands, were these words: "Victory or Death for Dixie."

Robert Hope, who had been searching for Sunny Withers since daylight, rode up and dismounted. The Confederate General saw, from his swimming eyes, that he knew the dead, and handed him the white handkerchief, the New Testament and the little red flag. Not a word was spoken, and, while Robert Hope was kneeling and sadly looking into the dead face, the General and staff silently rode away.

The remains were carried with the advancing army to Frankfort for interment. A Confederate officer placed the white handkerchief over his face; his mother laid the little Testament on his bier; . . . . dropped the bloody flag into the grave, and the rattling clods soon covered him. "Ready!" cried the Confederate officer, in clear tones: "Present. Fire."

The military salute reverberated over the waters of the beautiful Kentucky and died away among the cliffs and hills of Kentucky's public tombs.

Then they left him to rest under the blue sod in the shadow of Kentucky's battle monument.

Brief glory!

XIII.

THE Union army broke camp at Nashville and the famous race of '62 began between Bragg and Buell, the goal being Louisville.

Lema Sayr gathered all the lint, bandages and medicines left of a supply sent to her from New England.

In an ambulance furnished by General Bright, she followed the army, keeping close in the rear of the Seventh brigade, commanded by General Lytle, who composed the song "Cleopatra." In the excitement of the swift march, she maintained her presence of mind and safely avoided every peril.

Having arrived at Louisville, she went immediately to the hospitals. While visiting the cots at Ninth and Broadway she asked, "Why are the windows kept fastened and fresh air, so essential to the sick, excluded?"

"Because a rebel by the name of Hope prized one open and escaped over the roof," said the provost guard.

"Show me where he did it!" she exclaimed in a quick, nervous way that caused the guard to scan her face.

The soldier's manner called her attention to the interest she had manifested, and, with affected indifference, she said, "O never mind," but continued to think that it might have been *Robert* Hope.

After examining and noting the condition of every cot, saying kind words to one and giving little delicacies to another, she descended the two long stairways and spoke to the surgeon in charge about some sanitary changes the wards and rooms needed.

"Have you had many escapes, Doctor?"

"Only three since a man by the name of Robert Hope, whom we thought was ready to die, broke the window and escaped over the roof where a well man would have broken his neck."

She laughed at the doctor's way of giving her this information. He, too, like the soldier, looked at her face rather inquisitively, but his glance fell back repulsed and his unformed suspicion obtained no hold upon his mind. She bade him good afternoon and left.

While walking away she examined her nervous condition. She thought something must be wrong as her tone had drawn upon her the gaze of inspection successively from two strangers—evidently not psychologists. Mental drill on self-possession was going on when she met Capt. McCook, who had been promoted for gallantry on the field.

"May I have the pleasure of escorting you wherever you may be going?" he asked, so losing his self-control as to render his accents tremulous.

"You may and I am glad to have you do so," she gently replied.

Her tones seemed to say, "The soul from which we come is struggling for improvement and for a wider development."

He gazed into her blue eyes, which appeared to speak and like the tones of her voice to unfold purity and purpose.

"Do you know," said he, "that the soul can grow and expand, receive strength, polish and power from education in a greater degree than the mind or the body, subjecting both to itself?"

"I am no psychologist, but I hope it is so, for necessity requires some power to be connected with vile thoughts of the mind and weakness of the flesh, to control them."

"That necessity is supplied by the soul and the problem of life can be solved," said he abstractedly.

"What is *the* problem of life?"

"Education of the soul," was his sententious response.

"How can the soul be educated?"

"The soul," said he, "is the power which operates in the heart just as the mind is the power which operates in the brain. Brain is the thought producer and heart is the passion producer. If the soul be truly educated it will fill the heart with virtue, which, practiced exclusively, solves the problem of life."

"Is the soul physical?" questioned she.

Pausing a moment, he continued: "The physical being is visibly affected by the soul. You have but to study an angry countenance and a loving face, side by side, to see that. The heart would die if the soul were out of it. The letter killeth but the spirit maketh alive. The soul is so coupled with physical life as to keep the heart and brain sentient and active until worn out or destroyed by accident, perversion or disease. The soul is that mysterious thing called life. It does not reside out of the body. It resides in it. The physical ceasing to live, the intangible, pervading, essential and indestructible soul departs, freed from the flesh and its vices."

"Tell me, what is the final destiny of the soul?" she asked.

"The Savior alone can answer you, I can not."

"Then," said she, "on this point the world must trust alone to faith in the poor Carpenter of Nazareth."

"I do not believe it will always be so, for spiritual physiology will some day be quite as well understood as physiology of the mind and body, though science is not yet that far on the highway to truth; then Christ's doctrines will be demonstrated to the senses of the mind as well as to the faith of the heart. The spirit is to the mind and body what electricity is to the universe. No man yet knows his own intangible capacity, nor the powers of the air nor the strength of the incorporeal nor the power of moral force, which are things as much as the material world."

They had reached the boarding-house of Lexie Hallen's aunts, on Brook street, where Lema had secured rooms and meals by the week.

"I thank you, Captain McCook, for the pleasure

your suggestions on the soul have given me and beg to bid you good afternoon."

He had not said one word in behalf of himself, but wasted all the precious walk and its opportunity in airing favorite speculations. Confusion marked his leave-taking and his lingering glance at her calm, blue eyes and pure face laid bare the perturbations of his own soul, which seemed not to be a part, but the whole, of his physical being just at that moment.

"Lexie," said Lema at the dining table, "the army unexpectedly moves toward the heart of Kentucky day after to-morrow and I must go with it. Will you help me to get off."

"Yes," said Lexie, "if you will promise to take care of a Confederate by the name of Robert Hope, should you ever find him wounded."

Lema started and blushed at the sudden mention of his name, and for the first time seemed to feel the true condition of her heart. Instantly she began a mental reconnoisance, and, with the tendency to self-deception uppermost, she concluded that her blushes and uneasy demeanor came from nervous overstrain.

But Lexie was practical in her observations, and followed up the breach she had accidentally made with the statement that "Robert Hope is the noblest, bravest, handsomest man on earth. I believe I love him, and, Miss Sayr, your blushes at the mention of his name makes me think you love him too. Now, don't you? Where did you ever see him? Tell us all about it," and so the glib tongue of the Kentucky girl rattled away amid peals of laughter from the guests at the table.

"Oh, hush, Lexie," said her Aunt Bina, whose keen glance had discovered Lema's agitation.

This assistance gave the latter's heart, which had in it none of the subtilty dispensed in Eden, time to recover from the shock produced by Lexie's love alert suspicions, and she laughingly replied, "I will tell you all about him if you will go with me till we find him wounded."

"I will do it, if Aunt Bina will let me."

"Hush, child, you are too young for such risks," said her aunt.

"O do let me go, Aunty, I want to go so bad, just to help wounded rebels get away. Please let me go," pleaded Lexie.

At that moment a newsboy shouted, "Here's your Extra! General Nelson shot dead!"

Consternation emptied the seats about the dining table and all rushed to the door. A paper was bought. There it all was! One General had slain another on the same side for personal insult. The big, bluff, brave soldier, who, in a hailstorm of balls, had cursed the stampeded soldiers of Shiloh and Richmond, died in fifteen minutes from a pistol ball fired on the stairway of the Galt House.

All was excitement, hurry and anxiety on the first of October, as the left wing of Buell's army, under the brave McDowell McCook, took up its march along the Taylorsville road, followed by Gilbert in the center and Crittenden on the right, filling the Taylorsville, Shelbyville and Bardstown Pikes with fifty-eight thousand soldiers. Great clouds of dust rose over the way these mighty columns were moving and almost suffocated the soldiers, parched with thirst and choked with dust.

In the midst of the dust and the tramping and the confused hum of this advancing host, just in the rear of Rousseau's fated division, Lema rode in her unpretentious ambulance, which was filled with bandages, lint, medicines and wine. Lexie was by her side, her aunt having yielded to Lema's sweet persuasion and the promise of an early return to Louisville. She had said to the aunts that a battle was not expected, that it would only be a trip through the Bluegrass, and that Lexie needed an outing for a few days. The aunts had conferred privately, agreeing that Miss Sayr was an angel of goodness; besides, General Bright, Major and Mrs. Paymento had called to see her and would be along, and that she was, evidently, high in official favor. They had also discovered that Captain McCook escorted her to the house just before the dreadful news of General Nelson's death at the hands of General Jeff. C. Davis. So Lexie was permitted to go.

General McCook, ready to sacrifice all to glory, marched with his staff at the head of the plucky 15th Kentucky Infantry, destined by its list of dead to rank as the Union's bravest on Chaplin's Hills of blood and woe. The center corps was in position on the evening of the 7th. Then was the opportunity for the Confederate attack, but it was lost. That corps could have been crushed before McCook arrived.

At ten o'clock of the morning of the 8th of Kentucky's beautiful October, when the locusts, the crickets and the grasshopper were singing in the shocked corn and dying weeds and insects filled the browning woods with stridulous sounds, and approaching Indian summer in its smoky curtains brooded over cornfields, pastures and the broken woods that skirted the banks of Chaplin River's dead and dried currents, McCook's corps, Lytle's brigade on the right and Starkweather on the left, formed with its twenty-five regiments and thirty-six pieces of artillery on the crest of the rugged hills that lay behind the valley lands which reposed between them and the dry channel of the river.

Five hundred yards to the right of McCook, Sheridan's Division of twelve regiments and twelve cannon occupied the wooded ridges, swells and breaks in front of the Confederate left, overlapping it. Gooding's four regiments and Wisconsin battery shortly took perilous position in McCook's line. To the right of Sheridan stood General Robert Mitchell, with eight regiments and three batteries. In close order the First Division arrayed its fifteen regiments of infantry, eighteen cannon and First Ohio Cavalry ready to reinforce either wing or advance to the attack. Five regiments and one company of cavalry finished the dread array. Twenty-two thousand seven hundred additional infantry were moving on the Lebanon road only eight miles away, and would arrive before night. Thus sixty-four regiments of infantry, eighty-two pieces of artillery and six regiments and one company of cavalry stood in line of battle at 12 o'clock M.—thirty-five thousand three hundred strong, with twenty-two thousand seven hundred near at hand, within two hours' quick march, that is within supporting distance.

Down in the dry bed of Chaplin river, by the verge of its glazed, still pools, a gray line with bright bayonets was formed under the low projecting banks. A fine position for defense against a front attack but a slaughter pen in the event of a successful flank movement, which could have been easily made by the right wing of Gilbert's corps or Crittenden's approaching mass. The Confederate right wing was under that peerless soldier, Frank Cheatham, and composed of one Georgia and fourteen Tennessee regiments, numbering three hundred each, and eighteen cannon. Buckner was in the center with sixteen pieces of artillery and five thousand infantry, divided into four brigades; Anderson's division occupied the left, four thousand five hundred strong, with three batteries of six guns each. On the extreme right, Wharton's cavalry, one thousand strong, and on the left Wheeler's twelve hundred horsemen calmly awaited the onset.

Thus, at noon, stood fourteen thousand infantry with fifty-two cannon, four hundred and fifty cannoneers and twenty-two hundred horse—sixteen thousand six hundred and fifty soldiers—fronting thirty-five thousand three hundred, who were avoiding a general engagement until Crittenden's corps should arrive on the field to assist in pitched battle with the little Confederate army that stood proudly awaiting the fray and inviting it.

One o'clock came, and no advance upon the Confederates! Two p. m. struck by the clocks in the village of Perryville, and the gray line emerged from its cover, the right marching by brigades in echelon quickly formed line of battle and assailed the Federals posted behind limestone walls, in thickets, ravines, on broken heights, hills and precipices, behind trees, in skirts of woods, to the rear of open fields—in a position well nigh impregnable.

The resistance the Confederates met was firm and savage. Musketry and artillery slew whole companies at a single discharge! But they pressed up to the blazing muzzles. Buckner, under Hardee's orders, advanced, and, by the daring of his assault on the enemy's center, quite redeemed himself from that big scare Grant gave him at Fort Donelson, which cost the young Confederacy its brightest jewel on the waters and opened the way for gunboats which soon broke in twain the premature nation.

Cheatham having become hotly engaged, Bushrod Johnson and Pat Cleburne dashed with destructive impetuosity against the salient angle of the enemy's line at the crossing of Doctors creek. Wood, Brown and Jones obliqued to the right with their brigades and joined Cheatham's left. Colonel Sam Powell and Brigadier General Dan Adams from the Confederate left assailed Sheridan's division, and, diverging to the right, united with Cleburne. Wharton's cavalry charged with great fury, riding over stone walls, ravines, fences, through woods and up to McCook's infantry on his left flank, completely turning it. Wheeler, on the left, was aggressive, daring, watchful, ready to charge at the first sign of disorder among the foe.

The whole Confederate line, thus united, amidst the thundering of the artillery of both armies, moved to the bloody attack with intense ardor, cheers of defiance and indomitable pluck. Cleburne, Donaldson, Steward, Powell and Adams went straight at the salient and Sheridan's left front.

Liddell's brigade, having brought on the fight, was withdrawn and held in reserve until the supreme moment. Then its commander wedged it between Cheatham's left and Brown's right. There Bishop Polk was leading, and, in the twilight that was falling on the scene and in the dense smoke of battle, rode into the disordered lines of the enemy, but amidst the confusion and darkness instantly escaped. Returning rapidly to his advancing line, he met Liddell's solid brigade. Pointing in the direction whence he came, he cried, "Fire!" and an unbroken sheet of flame relit the fading light, quickly followed by another; a third completed the rout. The Federals fled in wild disorder, but under the cover of night their commanders reformed them one mile to the rear, the Confederates, by reason of the darkness, having ceased the pursuit.

McCook, like Lucius Manlius, lost his baggage. His papers and colors were also captured.

The Confederates had fought the battle without

support, two hundred miles from their base of operations, yet, with one-fifth of their number lost, they lit their camp-fires on the hard-won field and planted their pickets in the teeth of the concentrating foe.

Six thousand eight hundred and eighty-four soldiers lay stretched upon the earth, dead or mangled; three thousand one hundred and forty-five Confederates, three thousand seven hundred and thirty-nine Federals.

"I was badly whipped," said McCook on oath before the Buell Commission, which exonerated that gentlemanly soldier from blame.

"It was done in sight of Gilbert's whole corps." Then the Confederates turned and whipped half of the latter within hearing of Crittenden's advance, seeking the field not so fast as Blucher nor so slow as Grouchy. Such daring! Massena fought not more recklessly at Saragossa nor Ney at Waterloo. The boldness of the General who ordered the attack excelled Napoleon's presumption in his first campaign in Italy. For absolute risk, for perfect faith in capacity to do the impossible, for pure, unquailing courage that mounted with the occasion, this depleted army of Confederates will live in history, its praises sung by pens of poets and its valor furnishing fittest themes to grace Kentucky's romantic pages.

XIV.

BY five o'clock Rousseau, flanked, was falling back, Jackson of Kentucky lay dead among his cannon, Lytle, wounded, was a prisoner, and thousands, sound and well at sunrise, were swathed in blood, yet Lema Sayr's ambulance hovered upon the rear while she ministered to the wounded sent thither.

The scene was awful, the cannon and musketry deafening. Every face that passed in retreat and every courier who sought Buell with dispatches told of defeat, disaster and ruin.

The brave woman marked it all, but resolutely stuck to her mission. She bandaged the limbs of scores and staunched great wounds with lint. Water and wine, while there was a drop to drink, were handed from the ambulance by Lexie.

Night and Crittenden had come at last, but the defiant Confederates were bivouacking among the slain and picketing within the sound of low and cautious speech.

Lema Sayr reported the exhaustion of her supplies to General Bright, who commanded Crittenden's crack division, and he promptly resupplied her ambulance. At midnight she approached the field again, finding here and there a wounded soldier who had limped to the rear or who was being carried from the field on a stretcher, from which the drops of blood dripped, dripped, like drops of rain dripping from eves after a storm.

She said, "Lexie, you are a fine little rebel, you have helped me so bravely."

"Thank you," said Lexie; "now won't you go through the pickets and help the poor rebels some?"

The throes of night were bringing forth the birth of morning. A lusty game cock sounded his brave notes from the barn of the white house of which McCook speaks in his report of the battle, and Lema, in reply to Lexie, said, "I will as soon as day breaks and we can do so."

"But they will be fighting again," sadly returned Lexie, whose young heart, from sight of blood, had grown sick.

The conversation ceased a moment as the waning moon descended in shrouds toward tree tops and broken outlines of that rugged region. Silence and remaining still caused Lexie, exhausted as she was, to fall asleep. Lema drew her head upon her lap and prayed to the God of battles for peace, for no more bloodshed, while the child woman slumbered.

In this position, the morning uncurtained the field, first looking with its gray eyes into the faces of the dead and then wrapping the wounded with its brightening mantle.

The Confederates had withdrawn! The Federals moved to the brows of the silent ridges overlooking

Chaplin's dry channel and still pools, on which the trees, inverted, mirrored themselves. Field glasses were at the eyes of Generals, Aids and Colonels scanning the hills, pastures, woods, farm houses and roads beyond.

Lema and Lexie drove quickly up to an eminence. The cavalry, away to their left in a fog bank of smoke and mist, were skirmishing with Wharton, who was covering the Confederate retreat. A squadron of Kentucky troopers, which had reinforced him during the night, was maneuvering for display on the ridges to the southward.

"Look!" cried Lexie. "See those three Union soldiers charging on two Confederates in the bed of the river by that big pool? Yonder," pointing with excitement to the movement.

Lema placed her strong glasses to her eyes and looked intently. Lexie strained her bright eyes upon the movements of the combatants. A hand-to-hand combat was about to take place.

Robert Hope and a captain had lingered in the dry bed of Chaplin river near a big pool of water, for a parting shot, while Wharton was slowly retiring up the slopes, firing as he went. Colonel Lail saw from an elevation the defiant position of the two gray Kentucky troopers.

Turning to a lieutenant and an aide-de-camp who had joined him in the reconnaissance he said, "Let us pick up those daring fellows." Down the slope and across the valley they dashed. When within eighty yards of the river, concealed by its banks from the Confederates, they came to a dirt road running parallel with the river and between fences. Leaping the fence next to them, they turned to the left and in a few flying moments reached the point where the road turned down the sloping banks to the river.

Robert Hope had ridden to the top of the river bank and saw the three gayly decked horsemen galloping across the valley a few hundred yards to his left.

"Captain," said he, "we will fight them here, they are only three to two," and immediately took his position to the right of the road and faced toward the rapidly approaching Federals.

The Confederate captain quickly spurred up the sloping bank and reined his gallant steed in the center of the road a few yards to the left and slightly to the rear of Robert Hope. They looked each other in the face for tokens of determination and exchanged those significant glances which flash from gallant eyes when noble deeds are to be done. Their trusty pistols, with three chambers unexpended, clicked, and the beautiful Kentucky horses, on which, like Knights of old, they sat to receive the impending attack, reared their proud heads and uneasily pranced beneath their riders. Around the right angle, where the road turned squarely to the river, whirled the brave Federals in a bunch.

"O," cried Lexie, "what splendid fellows! I am so excited!"

Lema kept her glasses carefully to her eyes and

held her breath. Her lips quivered, and, in low tones, "O God, it is Robert Hope!" escaped from the depths of her soul.

Colonel Lail singled him out and fired within fifteen paces. Robert Hope returned the fire and spurred his excited steed to closer quarters, while the unquailing Colonel advanced to meet him. Again the leveled pistols' deadly crack followed so closely that Robert Hope's was barely distinguishable as first. He had shot the Colonel's left epaulette from his shoulder and a bullet had clipped the rim of his own cavalry hat just above the silver star, at which the Union Colonel shot as it flashed in the commotion. The third aim was taken within three deadly paces, and, as Colonel Lail saw the steady, liquid black eye of Robert Hope flash along the barrel of his revolver, he knew his time had come, unless he surrendered.

Throwing his hands aloft, with his beautiful silver-mounted pistol glistening over his head, he shouted, "I surrender! I'm your prisoner!"

Their horses' bodies had lapped. Their left knees were touching.

"Hand me your pistol," demanded Robert Hope, slightly lowering his own.

Colonel Lail appeared to obey, but, while pretending to hand the pistol to his adversary, seized him by the left collar of his gray coat with the left hand, thrusting the silver-mounted pistol under his left arm fired upward and the powder burned the face which, but a moment ago, had relaxed its rigidness to a foe begging for quarter. He saw the gleam of contempt blaze from the maddened eyes of his generous antagonist whom he had missed. Lail's heart sank within him. The desperation born of unfair advantage foiled seized his soul and with redoubled strength he tried to hurl his adversary to the ground. But the fates were against him! Robert Hope was a skillful Kentucky rider not easily unhorsed. His pistol was at the temple of his wily foe; loud rang the last shot and Colonel Lail fell dead from the black stallion which had so proudly borne him into the fight. Lail's head caught, as he fell, in the reins of Hope's now unmanageable steed, which whirled and dragged the body into the pool below. There stood the Confederate captain, knee deep in water, with empty pistol, strangling into surrender the aide-de-camp whom he had seized and thrown from his horse during their desperate struggle. The lieutenant had been carried by his pampered horse, which, uncontrollable, fled at the first fire to the main road; but the firing having ceased, he urged his frightened horse forward. It was too late! The Confederate captain covered him with his empty pistol and Robert Hope shouted, "Surrender!"

The heart-broken lieutenant, not knowing their pistols were empty, submitted and was disarmed, saying, with tears in his voice, "You have killed my Colonel!"

Quickly the Confederate captain mounted and compelled the aid to do likewise. Hope, unbuckling the gold-hilted sword from the body of the dead colonel, remounted his war horse and they galloped away with the two prisoners, their horses and arms as trophies of soldierly prowess. Colonel Lail lay face upward in the worn channel of Chaplin river, and his black stallion, wildly neighing, flew over the adjacent fields to which he had escaped when his master fell.

As Hope and his companion, with their prisoners, rose into full view on the hither banks of the bloodstained stream, that part of the Union army which had witnessed the duel cheered their gallantry and Kentucky's typical Confederates waved their hats in courteous response and passed out of sight over Chaplin's hills, which were now at peace.

XV.

LEMA SAYR said, "What a cruel war this is, but what a famous one it will be in history! I did not believe, in my New England home, the Southern people were so kind, brave or just. I thought them semi-barbarians. I see the mistake of my people! Come, Lexie, let us go quickly to the wounded. These twenty minutes have been as many hours to me."

Lexie exclaimed, "My heart stood still while they fought! O! But I am proud of the rebels!"

"Hush, dear child," said Lema, and they hurried away to a knot of soldiers who were heaping up the dead for burial. The wounded, blue and gray, were to be seen intermingled in every direction. Some were restlessly rising on their elbows, then falling back; others were plunging about apparently without pain; most of these were dying. Every few minutes one of them would be still! He had begun the solemn round of endless silence! Cries for water, help, "O come quick," were heard on every hand, and Lema and brave little Lexie were here, there, everywhere, with wine, lint, bandages, camphor, water. Lexie saw that Lema made no discrimination between the wounded, whether in crimsoned gray or blood-blotted blue, and she vied with her Northern sister in her "blue compliments," as she afterwards called her assistance to the Federal wounded.

Lexie's aunts saw the daily papers the next morning after the battle and immediately departed for the field. They arrived at the improvised field hospitals during the night of the ninth and in great anxiety sought for Lexie and Miss Sayr. They found them in a big barn which was full of the wounded, and the aunts clasped Lexie in their arms, almost smothering her with kisses. They greeted Miss Sayr with silent affection and a little reckless handshaking; but the pale faces of the sufferers under the weird lights that flitted about the barn floor deterred them from greater demonstrations. They watched the work of the nurses for a moment and then said to Lema, "Let us help."

She replied, "Certainly. Here, you can help now," pointing to a wounded soldier just brought in.

The two aunts took him in charge and soon he was resting easy.

Though Lexie and her aunts were Southern to the core, humanitarianism had filled their hearts too and poured its spirit into their receptive natures. They "worked together for good," with swift caution, deft fingers, staunching wounds, quenching thirst, appeasing hunger, while speaking gentle words to the sufferers.

Oh, how sweet the words of woman, when home or humanity is the theme!

As they softly ministered to him, the poor Confederate, covered with wounds, thought of his far-away Southern home among the prairie flowers of Texas; of Louisiana's broad verandas clustered with vines and trembling with the oriole's melodies and the mocking bird's song; of the anxious inquiries for him his comrades would make; of the retreating army in whose brave ranks, thinned by bullets, he had been stricken down; of the inhospitable Northern prison that opened its black mouth to swallow up his existence: and, as these women silently prayed, the gallant Union soldier, with broken limbs and pierced body, surrounded by friends, saw a sweet vision; he saw the broad plains of Illinois, Indiana's waving wheat fields or Ohio's blue lakes. He was back at home! But these women, intently laboring, absorbed and tender, only beheld their wounds or heard their groans and went on with their labor of love, which, though often unrequited here, will be their immortal plea for redemption.

The next morning, leaving Lexie and her aunts in charge of the mangers where lay the wounded whose souls One born in a manger died to save, Lema went to the white house, designated by McCook in his official report, to see if she might be useful there. On the parlor floor moaned twenty or thirty wounded, Union and Confederate. Their mingled blood had gathered in little pools on the carpet and the ruddy drops sprinkled the door sill and made it slippery. Convulsed humanity was then pouring out tears and prayers, while contending Americans were mingling their shed blood on the altar of opinion; but the blood of our heroes, commingled on the fields of our civil war, at last mounted the throne of Liberty and gave it eternal life.

She looked about the room with her practiced eye.

"Captain McCook!" she exclaimed in alarm, with tender, trembling voice, "are you hurt badly?"

His bloodless face indicated an affirmative answer plainer than words could express. She knelt by his side and smoothed back the black hair that strayed over his white forehead. He looked into her sympathetic eyes and tried to mirror his spirit upon her pure soul, but she deflected the picture and returned his gaze with gentle humanity and stood before his eye of love, panoplied with the recollection of another. She looked carefully to the heavy bandages which wrapped his powerful thigh and dampened the cloth that covered the contusion on his left cheek. She poured from her silver flask, into a crate-like cup, a draught of wine, and, gently raising his head with her hand, not now so soft as when she left her New England home, placed the cup to his lips and he drank of it. The love in his heart overcame all pain, drove from his mind every thought of his mishap and struggled in spite of all to his lips.

"I love you, Lema Sayr, and hope to die of these wounds if you do not return it," said he, looking into her face with reckless tenderness and a threat that made her draw away and her heart tremble.

She could say nothing, no, not even for truth's sake, for the perilous stuff of which delicious or demon dreams are made and out of which love builds, unbidden and unnoted, its mansion in the soul, weighed upon her heart and confused its impressions begun without warning in Shiloh's church and almost finished to disclosure on Chaplin's hills of observation, whence the day before she had seen with terror and fascination the famous war duel of Kentucky.

"Answer me, I am resigned! Only tell me the truth that I may know the truth," said the faint voice of the sinking soldier, the reaction from the shock of wounds having been checked by this sudden display of feeling.

"I will answer you at Louisville" said she, for the thought that anticipated favor would nerve him to live if he loved her truly and aid his recovery, had had time to enter her mind, and for that reason she avoided his present importunity.

"Thank you," said he, "I will live till then 'enlarging upon all the fair effects of future hopes.'"

Now was the time to withdraw, and, running the gauntlet of several pairs of soldiers' eyes who had heard snatches of the conversation, she precipitately left the room, and, in trembling doubt and misery, with heavy step retraced her way to Lexie and her aunts.

The surgeon general had ordered all the wounded, able to bear it, to be moved to Louisville, and the work of preparation was already begun when she returned.

She knew Captain McCook would receive great care, for already his name was on the rolls of fame at Washington, sent thither for promotion because of valorous deeds done on the field.

Next morning wagons, ambulances, horses, carriages, buggies, in a long line, took up the march for the beautiful city of the falls. Lema and her assistants camped with the wounded until the last night before reaching Louisville. Then they hurried thither to prepare for their reception.

XVI.

PENN GRABBÉ left "Colonel" Patter and Fate Wolf in the woods of Branch county, to which they had flown from Big Hill the previous August, and made his way through Ohio and Indiana to Louisville, arriving at the latter place October 14th.

Major Paymento was found at his headquarters near to Fort Hill, and a somewhat stormy scene ensued between him and Grabbé when the latter presented his third itemized account for recruits and expenses, direct and incidental. The honest old Massachusetts paymaster had grown incredulous since Grabbé had last seen him. Experience had taught him that even Union men would cheat the Government, and that the spirit of speculation, bold and shameless, had filled bureaucracy at Washington with its scandals and with its temptations had lured field and staff officials into peculation.

"I will not allow the Government to pay you twenty-three thousand dollars for your pretended 'incidental expenses,' nor will I allow seven dollars a day for wagons, even if every woman in Kentucky, who is not already one, should turn to be a rebel. Besides, the Government should no longer tolerate a contract which places men and live stock on the same footing," said Major Paymento to Penn Grabbé.

The latter sat self-poised while the old Major fretted in tone, and emphasized with "noise and emication" his last expressions, but, when he ceased and the air of the room was cleared of its blue tinge, Grabbé said, in injured tones, but with the greatest apparent kindness, "I want nothing from my Government, Major Paymento, which is not right! Here are the affidavits of 'Colonel' Patter, Fate Wolf, Eph Soaks and other good and reliable loyal citizens of Branch county, proving every item of my account to be just, due and unpaid. Yet I will not insist on my rights. If the Government needs it worse than I do, I will give you a clear receipt here and now and refuse to take one cent."

"O, well, I did not mean that," said Major Paymento.

"But whether you meant it or not, your language touched a tender spot and I now decline to take one cent of this account."

The old Major thought surely he had unjustly judged this hard-working friend of the Government and proposed to re-examine his accounts and do what was right.

Grabbé said, "Well, just to please you, Major, not that I want a cent of this account, you may do as you like," and took his departure, agreeing, however, to return next morning for final adjustment.

Hotel bills were high in the city, speculation having put them, with everything else, up to "war prices," and Penn Grabbé's prudence led him to seek lodgings in a boarding house. He was told that the

Misses Hallen, on South Brook street, kept one of the best at very reasonable rates. Thither he went, on the same evening that Lema Sayr, Lexie and her aunts arrived from the field of Perryville.

General Bright and Mrs. Paymento were calling and Grabbé quietly remained in the reception room, awaiting their leave-taking.

Lema was relating, in the unvarnished language of New England, the incidents of the great battle. She dwelt on Lexie's courage, judgment, kindness, skill and spirit. But, turning particularly to General Bright, she said, "She is a strong little rebel, though, and as honest in that belief as I am in mine. General, I hardly understand that; do you?"

"Yes," said he, "it is as natural as the unity of the suitable or the love of woman for the daring. Nature, blood, interest, association and sympathy have made the best Southern people one, and Lexie could not help being a rebel were she to try."

"That is so," said Mrs. Paymento, "for I have been thrown of late with Nashville ladies, who are refined, educated, charming, but they are the most intense rebels. It is a pity to kill men born of such women, for like mother like son the world over. I can scarcely forgive General McCook, brave as he is, for wanting to burn that beautiful city, because its women were intense rebels, and then retreat north. This is not a war of treason, and he knows it. It is a war of politics brought on by sectional, selfish and quarreling politicians and cranky philanthropists. Everybody on both sides is for republican government, except bounty jumpers, pension agitators, speculators and demagogues; and they would be for George the Third himself to gratify their cupidity. I wish it would end with all the States back in the Union so the respectability and courage of the South could have a fair chance free from the burden of slavery."

"Ah," said General Bright, laughing, "the same old result! . Whenever a Northern woman goes South and gets acquainted with the ladies she becomes an enthusiast over their accomplishments and at once a Southern sympathizer."

"I do sympathize with that noble people, even if they are in the wrong."

"But they are not in the wrong," chimed in Lexie.

"Now, you see, Mrs. Paymento, you are giving aid and comfort to treason," cried General Bright in great cheerfulness, laughing merrily.

"Come here, you darling, they shall not tease me or you either," said Mrs. Paymento, drawing Lexie to her side and caressingly adding, "You waited on the Union wounded at Perryville, and Miss Sayr says you did good service too, and you did, did you not?"

"Yes, I paid lots of blue compliments, lots more than gray ones."

"Why did you do that?" asked Mrs. Paymento.

"Because there were more of them," returned Lexie, casting, at the same time, a keen twinkle toward General Bright.

"Never mind, Lexie! Never mind, Lexie," said the General, rising to go, "we will get even with you yet."

"O, General, you ought to have seen that duel between two Confederates and three Yankees."

"How did it end?" he inquired.

"Humph! The rebels whipped, of course. Just get Miss Sayr to tell you about it. It was equal to the fight in Ivanhoe. One of the rebels fought like the Black Knight. He had red hair, though. I am going to call him the Red Knight. Miss Sayr was saying something to herself all the time during the duel. I believe she was praying, for I heard her say, 'Oh God,' as if her heart were breaking. I was excited to death! I was so afraid that I wouldn't get to see it all, and that the rebels would get killed! O! when one of them threw up his hands, dropped them again, and they seized each other, I thought I would die of excitement! Fights in novels are nothing! That excitement was ecstatic!"

General Bright stood as one riveted to the spot during Lexie's rapid description. Lema's color changed and mounted with red flags to her temples; all looked deeply attentive. To avoid any more of it, Lema said, "General, I will give you a full description of it when my nerves get settled."

"Thank you," returned he. "We must be going, Mrs. Paymento," and they withdrew with that courtesy which attends natural refinement.

"Who is the gentleman in the sitting room?" inquired Aunt Bina.

"I don't know," said the servant boy, Ned; "he didn't give me no cyard."

Aunt Bina went to see, and soon Penn Grabbé,

preceded by Ned, passed up to a room on the third floor. At supper Grabbé kept quiet, but observant. Next morning he could no longer forego his penchant to ask questions, and, after putting a good many astonishing interrogatories to those who sat in easy ear shot, finally, elevating his tone, asked Lexie, "Who is *your* sweetheart?"

"He is a man who don't ask questions," returned Lexie in the most nonchalant way to the great mortification of her aunts, who, though now poor, were beautifully educated and possessed refined manners.

Lema laughed a little to turn the wire edge of Lexie's answer, but thought, "He deserved it."

Grabbé awkwardly arose from the table, but lingered while asking some wholly useless information as a ruse to cover his retreat.

The ladies laughed, chatted and kindly aided him to get away with the best grace possible.

"Lexie, you naughty girl," said Aunt Bina, "you should treat every one with courtesy."

"But, auntie, how could I stand him asking you a long rigamarole of questions about our family and personal affairs?"

"But, dear, he did it innocently; to make conversation; just to be entertaining."

"No, he didn't," said Lexie; "he was gratifying his Yankee curiosity, and nothing else, at the risk of destroying everybody's appetite for breakfast," and then she petulantly ran out of the dining room. In a few minutes, her voice, soft and full, was heard from the upper hall, singing:

A PATRIOT'S STRATEGY. 131

"In the land of sun and flowers,
  His head lies pillowed low;
No more he'll cheer the Southern hearts,
  O! Zollicoffer, O!"

Lema said, "Did you ever hear such pathos in a human voice?"

The song died away and all disappeared to their rooms or duties.

Little did that family know of the impending trouble then gathering about their unprotected heads.

On the ninth of the preceding July, "Boil" Bridges was informed that the escape of Robert Hope took place the night two maiden ladies and a young girl had entered the hospital on his passport. He suspected, from that circumstance, they had aided the prisoner. In order to be sure of his victims, however, he had sent for a practiced spy and also a professional informer, and told them to work up the case. But the sudden irruption of Morgan's Confederate Cavalry, nine hundred strong, suspended detective operations and turned the attention of "Boil" Bridges to weightier matters. He began telegraphing at once to Lincoln, Buell, Stanton and subordinates everywhere for help. For convenience, the choice thoughts of his dispatches are condensed and are here presented in chronological order:

"LOUISVILLE, July 10, 1862.
President Lincoln:
  Kentucky will be overrun! Morgan has invaded the State with 10,000 men! All the rebels will join him! The State will be desolated! Send reinforcements! I have only four thousand available troops.   B. BRIDGES."

"LOUISVILLE, July 12, 1862.

Secretary Stanton:

Morgan whipped our troops at Lebanon. Louisville is in danger! Send cannon and troops! If I had enough troops I could hold him straight. I am not excited; the danger is really awful! The rebel citizens are laughing at us! B. BRIDGES."

"LOUISVILLE, July 14, 1862.

A. Lincoln, President, &c.:

What do you intend to do? The rebels are thicker than Falstaff's blackberries. Morgan robbed a bank! Burnt a bridge! He is murdering and stealing everywhere! His force increases; the villain will capture all my scattered troops. For God's sake, send troops. B. BRIDGES."

"WASHINGTON, D. C., July 14, 1862.

Gen. Halleck:

They are having a stampede over in Kentucky. It reminds me of a joke. I will tell you the next time I see you.
                                        A. LINCOLN."

"LOUISVILLE, July 17, 1862.

A. Lincoln, President, &c.:

I have telegraphed all the Adjutant Generals and Colonels at Washington to tell you to help us, but get no answer. I don't know where Morgan is; he has the best horses in the world; only the low and evil will join him. Fire and sword! An aid just in says Morgan is burning up the State! Killing all ages, ranks and sexes! Covington is rising against us! Do send reinforcements! I'll pay the stay-at-home rebels for this! Fighting at Cynthiana! God help us! You won't!
                        Persuasively,
                                        B. BRIDGES."

"LOUISVILLE, July 18, 1862.

Gen. Buell:

The villain Morgan whipped our troops at Cynthiana yesterday! I'll pay his uncles for it after he leaves. I will seize horses from secessionists and make them pay for rebel doings. Send reinforcements! No citizen shall hold an office in Kentucky. They are stealing horses again! No man ever had such times! The rebels spread every possible lie! Louisville is rising against us! Send troops quick!   B. BRIDGES."

Gen. Buell at this point telegraphed him:

"It is not proper to war on citizens or levy contributions upon them for opinion's sake.   D. C. BUELL."

"LOUISVILLE, July 21, 1862.

Gen. Buell:

A more vigorous policy must be pursued. Morgan has burnt another bridge! Do please, for Heaven's sake, send reinforcements. All is lost! With fair officers I could take Morgan, but Ward and G. Clay Smith are no account. If I only had officers! Don't you want G. Clay Smith? He ought to be a Baptist preacher and predestinate the rebels to eternal damnation. Do take him off my hands! He got in sight of Morgan yesterday and let him get away, surrounding two stragglers by forming a hollow square. O the martinet! He should be shot for precision.   B. BRIDGES."

"LOUISVILLE, July 24, 1862.

Secretary Stanton:

Lincoln and Buell are unappreciative, and I therefore telegraph you. Now, just look at this dispatch from Morgan to me: 'Good morning, 'Boil.' The telegraph is a great institution. You should destroy it, as it keeps me too well posted. I have all your soldier-like (?) dispatches. Don't destroy bridges or railroads; I have attended to that. Keep cool!' What a villain he must be! I'll hang his operator for it if I catch him. See how my patience is tried.   B. BRIDGES."

"LOUISVILLE, July 25, 1862.

A. Lincoln, President, &c.:

Morgan is gone! His uncles and rebel citizens shall pay the damages done by him! I would suggest as good policy you issue a proclamation for a national thanksgiving and remove G. Clay Smith from the field of war. B. BRIDGES."

The following dispatch closed the electrical correspondence:

"WASHINGTON, D. C., July 26, 1862.
Gen. Buell:
Am in doubt whether 'Boil' Bridges is an incompetent patriot or the worst product of civil war. Restrain him. Old Kentucky is my native State! A. LINCOLN."

No sooner had Morgan gone than news of the approach of General Bragg's army threw "Boil" Bridges into an effervescent state. Utter consternation followed, and other officers were at once put in command. Thenceforward "Boil" Bridges ceased to be conspicuous. His professional informer had turned rebel during the Confederate occupation of Kentucky, and his spy was no more. Thus the clouds that hung over Lexie and her aunts were pushed away, and "Boil" Bridges sank into that oblivion which now well nigh covers him from verbal criticism. But his cruelty, recorded in black characters on Kentucky's pages of history, can never be obscured.

From this historical retrospect I will now return to the thread of Penn Grabbé's strategitical life.

XVII.

"GOOD morning, Major Paymento," and Penn Grabbé seated himself, saying, "Major, I have thought over my claims against the Government, and concluded to leave the whole matter to you."

"But, sir, I can take no such responsibility," returned Major Paymento. "You must submit this item of 'Incidental Expenses' to the Bureau at Washington, I am ready to pay you for recruits and any *live stock* for which the Government may owe you."

For the first time in his life Penn Grabbé was circumvented by honesty, but, assuming the countenance of virtue, he said, "Strike out the 'Incidental Expenses' and put the wagons at two dollars and fifty cents per day, your own estimate at the time I told you rebel women fixed the prices and—"

"Humph! Go on to other matters, I want to hear no more about rebel women, but more of honest dealings with the Government," said Major Paymento in a tone of Massachusetts granite.

"I was about to remark," coolly said Grabbé, "that I guessed I ought to be satisfied, though not compensated, with any settlement you would make, and that I am willing to take twenty-three thousand dollars in final settlement for the horses, mules, cattle and recruits furnished by me up to date."

Major Paymento had scrutinized the account during the previous night, and with some suspicion said, "Can you tell me, sir, why you are willing to lose twenty-three thousand dollars for 'Incidental Expenses' and cut down the remainder of your account almost half?"

The ingenuity of Penn Grabbé was here put to a severe test, but his early mathematical training came to his relief and he answered: "First, I wish to quit the unpleasant and dangerous business of recruiting; second, I bought the mules, horses and cattle in my account under a trade permit from 'Boil' Bridges at half price from rebel sympathizers who were afraid of confiscation or imprisonment; third, I made on a former contract thirty thousand dollars; and, lastly, these statements will show any candid man that I have made seven thousand dollars clear, if my loss for Incidentals be excluded."

This seemed to satisfy Major Paymento, and the account was settled on the lump basis. Penn Grabbé received a check therefor and departed with a bit of cold courtesy. He remained in Louisville ten days for the purpose of becoming acquainted with the regimental brigade and division quartermasters and commissariats. When he left he knew them all. On arriving at Cincinnati he lodged at an obscure hotel and became acquainted with a Jew clothier by the name of Habbakkuk Wallenstein. After several days' conversation, in which profits on army contracts of every kind were discussed, biblical knowledge exhibited and cross-analysis of character made, Penn Grabbé became convinced that Habbakkuk Wallenstein was the sort of man he was seeking. By this time the Yankee and the Jew tendency to make acquaintances had put them on a friendly basis, and each became communicative to the other.

Penn Grabbé said, "I have cleared one hundred and twenty-six thousand dollars during the last twelve months," and Habbakkuk Wallenstein declared, without meditation, "I haf cleart twice dat much."

Penn Grabbé, continuing, said, "Then if you and I wished to do so, we could fill a big clothing contract on half of our capital."

"Vel, I tink so," said Habbakkuk, "but you vil haf to put up de monies and I vil furnish de cloding," the fact being that he had made four assignments, been burnt out twice, lost the insurance because he dared not sue the Insurance Company, and was at that moment overwhelmingly, but not hopelessly, in debt.

In legal phrase, the *aggregatio mentium* took place between them. Penn Grabbé exhibited a genuine contract with a quartermaster of the army, dated at Louisville, for the supply of thirteen thousand uniforms at twenty-one dollars each and twenty thousand army blankets at five dollars apiece.

Habbakkuk's eyes nearly popped out of his head. From that moment obsequiousness, apparently perfect trust and great admiration for Penn Grabbé marked every word, look, smile and act of Habbakkuk. Now and then he declaimed the eloquent Third Chapter of Habbakkuk with piety and precision. Grabbé listened to this innocent soul until he beheld a child-like trust that quieted every doubt and gained his full confidence.

On Christmas day following their agreement Habbakkuk had the uniforms and blankets ready to ship. He wrote for Penn Grabbé to come at once. The latter received the letter, and, abridging both time and space, arrived at Cincinnati within twenty-four hours.

The clothing and blankets were sent to Nashville marked C. O. D., and Habbakkuk insisted, although Grabbé had proposed to go alone, that he too should go along to explain away any objections to the clothing that might arise.

Nothing, however, happened to disturb the smooth machinery which Penn Grabbé had oiled in his own way, and the quartermaster drew his draft on the Government for three hundred and seventy-three thousand dollars, payable to Wallenstein and Grabbé.

"Dat sheck shoot not be casht here," said Habbakkuk; "it shoot be sent by de Attums Expriss to my bankers, Bloomgold ant Levi, ant save us from bein' robt."

"I agree with you," rejoined Grabbé, and it was forwarded as suggested by Habbakkuk.

Arriving at Cincinnati late the next evening, Habbakkuk would listen to nothing but that Grabbé should stay at his private residence that night. This residence belonged to Bloomgold and was extraordinarily furnished, exhibiting, in mixed profusion, marks of social taste and a peddler's brassy pen chants; but Habbakkuk claimed the house as his own and made Grabbé believe it.

They had goose, fattened in the cellar while its webbed feet were nailed to a plank, for supper and three kinds of wine. The talk lasted far into the night. The mildewed clothing, rotten fabric of the army overcoats, second-hand blankets and general cheating practiced on the Government, were gone over in great hilarity. They drank to each other frequently and fully. When it was growing late, Habbakkuk said, "De rebel bullets wilt shlip betwent de stitches uf dem overcotes ant de breeches vilt last dem vun vweek undt ve vilt selt dem som more."

This tickled Grabbé immensely.

"How much profits do you suppose, Habbakkuk, we have made?" asked Grabbé, rising to go to bed.

"Vel, I shoot say—bout tree hundret tousand dollars."

"I will bid you good night on that," said Grabbé, taking the lamp from Habbakkuk's hands at the door of the room to which the latter had conducted him.

Grabbé was told to sleep late, as the household breakfasted at ten, and that he must meet "Mrs. Wallenstein mit de babie;" besides, "de bank vilt not be opent tilt leven."

Grabbé prayed that night for divine grace to sustain him in his renewed resolution never again to engage in questionable dealings with his Government, or risk his earnings by entering on other ventures.

He promised his Maker that he would build a soldier's widow and orphans' home in Branch county when peace should be declared, and thus he sought to atone for misconduct which seemed to his conscience to result from the nature of the war. He fell asleep, and with the quiet of confidence which Habbakkuk had inspired, passed a dreamless night and awoke physically refreshed. Habbakkuk had breakfasted and gone to the store, while a Jewess servant acted the part of Mrs. Wallenstein, leaving the baby, however, in the maternal bed to finish its prolonged slumbers.

Grabbé's suspicions were not aroused nor his appetite blunted, hence he ate heartily and was mentally happy! On the way to the store he loitered while enjoying a cigar and looking at officers' uniforms and trappings which lined the show cases of the Jewish quarters. Finally he reached Wallenstein's establishment, which was a dingy, narrow building in that quarter which lies to the west of Vine and south of Fourth, and called for the proprietor. He was answered by the clerk in charge that Mr. Wallenstein was out but would be in shortly. The clerk invited him to be seated. In response to his inquiry about business he was told that the house had given its employes a Jewish holiday; that, doing only wholesale business in army specialties, they often appeared to be shut down, when, in fact, they were simply resting up for other big contracts, the policy of the house being to reject all small deals.

Thus Grabbé was entertained until noon, when a

a keen pang of suspicion shot through his brain. Habbakkuk had not come. The establishment seemed to be abandoned. It had, all at once, a desolate appearance. Anxiety flushed his face and self-possession forsook him.

"Where is Wallenstein?" he sternly demanded of the frightened clerk, who had watched every change of feeling through unerring facial signs.

The clerk chattered, "I don't know, I don't know, I vilt go for him," and snatched his hat.

"No you won't," shouted Grabbé, violently seizing him by the collar. "You will go show me the banking house of Bloomgold and Levi!"

"Velt let me go ant I vilt go mit you," said the clerk.

Grabbé released his hold, and, stooping to pick up his hat, which had fallen off when he grabbed the clerk, he saw something like the flit of a bird toward the rear of the building. Rising and rushing after the flying clerk, he saw his form drop, as it were, through a trap door, and visions of wealth seemed to disappear with him. The banking house of Bloomgold and Levi was found; the Government draft had been received and honored, but Mr. Wallenstein, for some unaccountable reason, so Bloomgold said, had removed his deposits, both firm and individual, leaving the bank in total ignorance of his motive. Grabbé put private detectives on Habbakkuk's track, but the latter had not left a rack behind while folding up his existence in clouds of deep obscurity.

Returning to Branch county, after weeks of wasted

search, Grabbé retired to his farm and remained inactive during the rest of the eventful year of 1863. That year, beginning with President Lincoln's proclamation freeing the slaves, culminated with Gettysburg on the 3d and Vicksburg on the "ever memorable 4th of July," as "Colonel" Patter would say. It marked the highest tide of the flood of war which thence prevailed exceedingly in the stricken South until the ark of a new political covenant rested upon the plains of Appomattox. Thence the croaking raven winged its flight to the land of Reconstruction, while the dove of peace found no rest for the sole of her foot until the olive branch flourished in the hands of a thief who stole the Presidency "and put it in his pocket."

XVIII.

CAPTAIN McCOOK suffered intense pain and for a long time his life hung in the balance. Lema visited him regularly and was kind to him. Her gentle voice and considerate words cheered him, however, more than all else. They seemed to have a subtile influence over him, but his fond interpretation increased their power. What she did was from a different motive than assigned in the silence of his strong feelings. She saw he was misleading himself. She did not love, but honored him, and felt great interest in his welfare. She pitied him and suffered much for his sake. In her prayers she often asked for the gentlest means of undeceiving him. Her distress of mind grew with her inability to tell him the truth. Exhausted energies and unhappiness began to tell their old story in the fading light of her face. Her once springy step doubtingly touched the floor, the sound of her voice was dull and meaningless, the breezy spirit gone, and, weary laden, she seemed to sink under her burdens.

Captain McCook had not asked, either with tongue or pen, performance of her promise made to him at Perryville. He pleaded with his eyes and pledged his love through tones unmistakable in meaning, yet he never asked the question which she feared most and constantly anticipated. He showed plainly how well he loved her, but, like one playing for an inestimable prize, deferred casting the final die. The masonic sign of lovers had not been given him from the eyes, which speak with greatest power the soul's sacred mystery, nor had her tones betrayed any love for him. The absence of the lover's tokens the world over silenced his tongue, and, trusting to the mute persuasion of his mangled feelings, he hoped for favor which never came.

Lexie had become strongly attached to Lema and ran to meet her at the door whenever she returned from the labors of the hospital. She sat by her side at the table and watched her tired face as it grew wan from anxiety and overwork. None knew of her secret distress, and she sought no confidante in the affairs of her heart. Her appetite was gone, and the nerves, ready for rebellion at all times, like the people of republics when overtaxed, showed evidences of disorder. She was sick when she got to the house that cold December night on which the awful battle of Murfreesboro was begun, and Lexie's aunts at once gave her a hot bath and put her to bed. Lexie was set to watch and give the medicines at proper times and keep the damp cloth upon the aching head. At midnight a strong sedative became necessary. Soon the eyes, that had unselfishly watched over others so often, were closed in uneasy slumber which grew quiet after a while, and the morning was far gone before she awoke.

"I must go to my mother," said she, languidly arising from the long, restful sleep.

"O we will take just as good care of you as your mother, and you shan't go," pettishly said Lexie, who had not left her side during the night.

Aunt Bina came in, and, after a few questions and answers, saw that mental trouble and overstrain were telling upon the beautiful face and spirit.

"O, auntie, don't let her go."

"Hush, dear, be quiet!"

Lexie was silent, but gazed curiously at the changed face and parched, unmurmuring lips. Then her eyes filled with tears, the real condition of her friend having dawned upon her.

That evening General Bright and Major and Mrs. Paymento called to see Lema, and it was agreed she should start for home on the morrow.

The thoughts of her dear Massachusetts home and of her old mother and sisters, whom she had not seen for many months, revived her spirits and some of her wonted cheerfulness returned to enliven even Lexie's down-crushed spirits. Next morning she wrote Captain McCook a kindly note of farewell, and sent messages to the sick and wounded, who received them with silent tears or spoken words of sorrow, and prepared to depart for her Eastern home. She was accompanied as far as Indianapolis by Lexie and her Aunt Julia.

When they parted Lexie's red swollen eyelids and suppressed feelings, in dumb eloquence, said, "Good-bye"—a phrase so common, yet so rare.

linking the divided by its notes of love, or tones of friendship, or yet marking separation with convenience, or, the grave of a passing acquaintance with dead emphasis. Such is the varied power of these two monosyllabic nothings.

Such are human tones that the genuine stand for truth and love, while the false, from appearance to indifference, from selfishness to hypocrisy, are unerring signs of the absence of charity.

Lema breathed quickly, while she folded the brave, guileless girl in her arms, then mute, boundless in affection, with no thought of her own misery, she clung to her child friend until torn asunder by the rude scream of the iron horse. In thirty hours she was walking up the frozen walk between the leafless maples, and, in another moment, she was in the sweet home of her youth, with its talisman of virtue, its altar of faith and a mother's love.

Here her health returned, but, when the old happiness of home put in its appearance, her spirit was delirious with dread, for its scattered power no longer focussed itself upon the sun glass of home and its dear associations. A change had been wrought, and the form of the stranger, an enemy to her country and kindred, was present at every touch of the spring of recollection. The love of a patriot wooed her with its fit associations and fervid purity; while him, of her youth, she could no longer call from low estate to the uncrowned monarchy of a heart worthy of a prince; alas! the fountains of her heart had flowed into other channels, the limpid surface had been broken by rude winds, and the morning star of life glinted, undefined, in the waves which now rolled high on the sea of her altered existence. The world had been too much for her, but a new life had been molded out of materials of the heart and conscience by nature's master methods.

Throughout the year war news, the quality of the Southern people, their institutions, customs and civilization were among the themes of every evening's social converse around the broad old fire-place. After Lema became well enough to perform the task, she essayed to answer the repeated questions of her mother.

"I could not tell you all I saw, heard, thought and felt, dear mother, were I to talk of it the rest of my natural life. My experiences have shed another light on the Southern people. While I found them engaged in a useless war of politics, I discovered they were sincere, courteous and brave. All of them seemed to resent the idea that they were fighting against republican government. Their pride of ancestry, who may have been soldiers or statesmen, is excessive, but not to be compared with their love for the new Confederacy. At Nashville I was introduced to ladies of families that had furnished the soldiers of that city to the South, and I must admit they are spirited, patriotic, from their standpoint, and possess the manners of refined associations. The men woo women with the dash of mediæval knighthood, and their movements are marked by the pleasing dignity of high-born owners of baronies. At first I did not like this, it was so foreign to our plain, puritan manners. Nor did their homes, furnished apparently for effect, exhibit the thrift and economy which New Englanders love and enjoy. They have too much flourish, their blood is hot and their courage is sensational and not so steady as daring; but it all trends to the ideal, and, freed from the blight of slavery within the folds of a restored Union, a Union of preservation and not of conquest, they would rise to sublime heights of mental, moral and patriotic grandeur."

"My child," exclaimed the old mother, the white frills of whose cap encircled the high forehead crowned with spectacles, "how can you attribute morality to a people who own human beings and take their labor for nothing?"

"I have learned, mother, that our ancestors once did these same things, and that customs, manners, laws, traditions and conditions govern human conduct, and, as in the case of St. Paul, make men conscientious in evil, and, when enlightened, constructively great in action. The conscientious man, however wrong in his theories and practices, is the honest man. From these premises, constructed from history, the philosophy of life and my own experience, I have concluded that the South, though wrong, believes she is right; that her people, while warring against the inevitable, will share our victory at the end—for they are victors who are vanquished by their own errors—and leave behind them a more glorious military history than our own people. At

Nashville, they did good to their enemies, for they sent meat and drink to the wounded, nursed many of the sick in their own homes, while praying for their absent ones, their new government and those in authority over it. Mother, there is more humanity in the South than was ever dreamed of in our philanthropy. In the city of Louisville, I boarded with a Southern family which was visited a great deal by Southern people, and heard them talk. Their thoughts were worn upon their sleeves and no malice marred their hearts, Little Lexie Hallen, of whom I told you, would help a rebel escape in one moment, but in the next administer to the sick or wounded Unionist. They are a curious people to us, but none more lovable or brave exists. The Kentuckians are divided and the native Unionist is very hostile, and many of them barbarous toward the families of the Kentucky Confederates. It is a common thing to arrest old gray-headed men and bright, educated women, levy tribute on Southern citizens for acts of armed Confederates and speculate off of them by trade permits given only to Unionists. To cap the climax of folly and passion, the Union Legislature passed a law expatriating Kentucky Confederate soldiers and divorcing them from their wives."

"Oh, that is persecution," cried her mother, "and should be stopped by Mr. Lincoln at once. A Union, restored by such means, will leave open wounds to fester for a quarter of a century and mar our great philanthropic war forever."

The daughter, continuing, said, "I heard that he

had telegraphed last summer to that cultivated and highly civilized soldier, General Buell, to curb this element and restrain their viciousness, and I have hope it may be done."

She told her mother, day by day, parts of the scenes through which she had passed, of the manly character of Captain McCook, of Lexie's fidelity and childish candor, mixing into the narrative, with due caution, her experiences at Shiloh and the description of Kentucky's war duel. When she first mentioned Robert Hope's name it sounded so much like the announcement of his presence that her heart beat its excitement in her white throat and the quiver of her voice attracted her mother's curiosity.

"What's the matter, daughter?" cried her mother, looking straight and searchingly into her face.

"O nothing!" gasped Lema; "I fear I have heart trouble."

"Yes, yes," said her mother. "I remember well how my heart used to jump into my throat and my voice tremble like an aspen whenever the name of a young man, who afterward became your father, was mentioned."

Lema, recovering, laughed at her mother's clinging vanity and talked of the girlish flippancy with which she alluded to her early courtship, until she made the mother's late-blooming conceit a little afflictive to her dignity. Thus Lema finally escaped from the effects of mentioning Robert Hope's name too suddenly and thenceforward became more circumspect in her references to him.

The conditions about the old home had changed and Lema's filial duty, as she understood it, demanded of her more sacrifices. Patriotism still burned brightly in her bosom, and, though deprived by circumstances of active work in the field, she determined to encourage with her pen the men of the Republic to save the Union, to save the South to it, to save liberty for mankind, liberty which honest differences had put to the hazard and which the war might destroy from the face of the earth forever.

XIX.

DURING Lema's long absence her mother and sisters had fallen in debt, and small creditors, as usual, were impudent, importunate and cruel.

The Sayrs, being intensely loyal to the Union, went beyond their ability in contributions to the cause. The small investments made before Lema's departure for the field of war had depreciated, and the old home was again in danger of being sold or mortgaged. To avert this calamity and protect her aging mother from want and her sisters from the oppressions of poverty, she was constrained to forego the great work of charity which she had so bravely begun.

While casting about for something to do, and meeting frequent disappointments, she was consoled to learn that the great Sanitary Commission was fully organized, and that sick and wounded soldiers would be cared for in a systematic way. But what could she do or get to do was the question to which she was forced to recur.

Finally taking up her pen, she wrote a story of the war based on her own experience and sent it to a Boston periodical. It was accepted, and a small etched check remitted to her in return for it. She looked at the beautiful check, turning it about in her hands, thinking of the possibilities of authorship. The wild scenes of the mighty struggle which she had witnessed arose to her mind; like an echo from memory's marvelous horn sounded the voices of the dim past, and a feeling of sadness settled like a mist at eventide upon her heart, ever ready for the blues or buoyancy as occasion dictated. The night of her life seemed to have come, but the music of an invisible charm arose, merry as a marriage bell, and floated through every chamber of her gloomy heart, and when its exquisite sounds died away she flung the reins to fancy and, as in a trance, felt the coming consolation which every woman longs for. She had learned of love and sorrow that the highest ethical joy springs from the ashes of the passions, and that contentment and human perfection are born of toil, care and duty done, hence she hoped and was willing to labor and to wait.

Then said she, "I will fasten a purpose to my soul and write literature until the robes of fame fall upon my shoulders and give to life a reputation which shall be prolonged after death."

Arising from her reverie she sought her mother, and laid in her wrinkled hand the first golden fruits of her pen. New life was in every movement then, for uncertainty of purpose no longer neutralized her energy.

First a cozy library was improvised in an odd room in one corner of the building. The wide wood fireplace, with its mantelpiece of black walnut, took up half of one side of the room. The low ceiling and brown walls were papered with figures of colonial times. A quaint little window, filled with eight little panes of glass, let in the light from the sea and placed its breakers under the eye of the restless occupant of this unpretentious apartment.

With her own hands, and the aid of her mother's spruce and tidy notions, she brushed, swabbed, wiped and cleaned the woodwork, window glass, stone jambs and slated hearth until not a dowdy spot smudged the interior of "Think." That is the name she gave it; pasted on each window pane, over the doorway and to the back of the maple-wood chair, sawed for her ancestors from the forest primeval.

"What books do you intend to put in Think?" asked her mother.

Lema meditated but a moment, then replied, "The Bible, Shakespeare, Webster's Dictionary, the latest edition of the best work on Anatomy, Botany, Geology, Astronomy and Chemistry. By these lights I can study God, Earth and Stars, Man and Flowers. I can extract a type and shadow of all evil and of all good from my own nature and my own experience. The rest I can trust to the unknown resources of the mind and the undiscovered capacity of the soul. With these aids added to the palpable senses, I think the brain might work wonders."

"But, daughter, you have left out Jonathan Edward's Sermons, the Catechism and Fox's Book of Martyrs."

"Yes, mother, for they contain too much of 'the horrible and awful,' and not enough of virtue's natural capacity to protect itself."

"O I fear," said Mrs. Sayr, "since you went South you have imbibed loose notions, and our good old New England faith has lost its charm for you. God help you, daughter, to return in mind and heart to our old ways." She left the room abruptly.

"Lema fell to thinking, and thought on until the falling curtains of night blinded the eyes of the little window and darkened Boston's waters. She dropped into an easy slumber for a moment and awoke with her aspirations half quieted. Next morning she was early in the library, and by noon it was ready for the books. In the evening she went to Boston and bought a chess board and ivory men and the best editions of her select library, save only the Bible, which is always at hand, old, used and revered, in every New England home.

In Think she wrote many living, breathing stories of the war over a *nom de plume*, and coined her thoughts into small money—into enough to bring subsistence and keep the roof free from mortgage. She was studious, at intervals dwelling upon the ideal, even when her heart was full of the exacting anxiety which fills every heart where debt and bread are always in sight of each other. The mental shadows, the transitions through which her thoughts and feelings had passed, were always before her eyes, and filled many of her pure pages with profound epigrams on human vicissitudes.

XX.

IN the absence of Penn Grabbé's devising mind, Fate Wolf's cunning and "Colonel" Patter's pedantic palaver combined for safety and profit. They did a big business in substitute traffic. Eph Soaks, having jumped the bounty from eleven different regiments under as many *aliases*, appeared in Fate Wolf's neighborhood. Two drafts had been ordered, and Kentucky's quota was 12,021. These observant patriots knew that the demand in military markets for substitutes would be great, and patriotically turned their attention in that direction.

The greater part of Penn Grabbé's recruits had come home, some had re-enlisted under other names and in different organizations, and some had even gone to other States with new names for those obsolescent designations under which bounties, blue clothes and green money had been drawn on more occasions than one.

Fate Wolf said: "The woods air a runnin' over with turrible good subter-shoots. Less us gather 'em in en hold a meetin' en vote to jine our hands ez a band uv brothers en make sumthin' ez other people air a makin'."

"Your plan is full of strategy, and means much to its followers." remarked "Colonel" Patter.

The ensuing Thursday night twenty-seven practiced bounty jumpers met at Fate Wolf's cabin, on Tippling Fork, to devise ways and means on the subject of substitutes.

Fate Wolf had occupied this habitation since his marriage in 1830 to Miss Scatlett Purvine. From the north the house is approached by a narrow pathway that leads through heavy woods and bushes until the bold cliffs of Tippling Fork are reached. They tower three hundred feet on either side of the clear stream which runs for twenty miles between them, through gorges so contracted at points that each drop of water crowds in for passage. It flows over white and yellow pebbles, glistening beneath its surface like pearls and opals. Now and then the wandering stream runs along narrow strips of land nestling at the foot of the lofty cliffs, which are at no point more than one hundred yards away from its purling, gurgling or still-flowing waters, that, at times, disappear amidst nature's sublimity. From the tops of the cliffs, the narrow path to Fate Wolf's cabin is a crevice in the rock that seems to have been cracked open by an earthquake. It is barely wide enough to admit one man. Half way down this dizzy descent the crevice stops, and a huge, unbroken ledge projects from the main wall of the cliff and breaks the passage for twenty feet. To overcome this obstruction, Fate Wolf had improvised a ladder of saplings and grapevines, disguising it with leafy branches. From its foot the descent is irregular and difficult until the base of the cliff is reached. There, from season to season, nestled among the verdure of spring, or the corn and wild flowers of summer, or the fading colors of fall, Fate Wolf's cabin sends up its blue smoke in spiral columns toward the milky way by night and the narrow strip of blue in the high heavens by day. There is a bridle-path which circles the ends of the cliffs seven miles below the cabin; but, where the path enters the rocky jaws of the gorge, it is lost in obscurity and a labyrinth of changes frequently made by Fate Wolf for "pertection" against intruders.

Here Fate Wolf's first great meeting as a band of brothers to consider the substitute business was held in the gloomy year of 1864. After an all night's wrangle over the personal risks about to be run and the safest way to avoid danger, Fate Wolf was selected to visit the richest centers of the State and make contracts with those drawing unfortunate lots in the draft. In less than a fortnight the twenty-seven substitutes had been placed at one thousand dollars each. A uniform, bright gun and glittering bayonet were in the hands of every man, and every man, like a new invention, bore a novel name.

Fate Wolf and "Colonel" Patter, after the business in hand was done, started back home, but, before reaching that bulwark of predatory freedom, Eph Soaks and half dozen more were there talking with Scatlett Wolf about other chances and hiding during the day among the cliffs of Tippling Fork.

Having divided their half commission, "Colonel" Patter and Fate Wolf sallied forth in search of other substitutes. They confined their movements, for prudential reasons, to the by-ways and cliffs of Tippling Fork and the dense woods of Catamount Creek.

One day they ventured from their exclusiveness into Roan, and Penn Grabbé, fortunately, was riding thither. Morgan and his men had passed through the town, threatening to burn it, scaring Union people and encouraging Southerners in like degree. The tavern-keeper, for the first time in his life, talked cautiously.

Fate Wolf and Penn Grabbé dismounted, and, seeming to sort together, retired to the stone steps of the closed Court House for a private conference. They conferred earnestly and on the shortest lines of strategy.

"Thar's lots uv money in subter-shoots," said Fate Wolf, his big, dirty blue eyes filling with tears as he laughed and told Penn Grabbé of the speed and cunning of certain substitutes who deserted the first night and beat him back to the cliffs and shades of Tippling Fork.

"I think them Catamount Crick fellers would make turrible good subter-shoots," he added.

Penn Grabbé patiently listened, but his strategic thoughts were absorbed in other prospects and ran ahead to future possibilities. His prescient mind had caught glimpses of the future's temptation to demagogues and the opportunities which a successful civil war would give for spoils through laws based on false clamors of patriotism, and while Fate Wolf pointed to fortune and how to make it, Penn Grabbé took in the future, anticipating its monster birth with miser hopes.

Having recovered from his alleged rheumatism, his mind recovered its natural activity, but his speculative heart, somewhat chastened by experience with Habbakkuk, bade him be content with safer chances and smaller profits than prevailed in previous ventures.

"Fate Wolf," said he, "your house will have to be the headquarters of this business. It is the only safe locality for it that I know."

"Alright! Ha! ha! ha! It'll swaller 'em up frum enny persooters," rejoined Fate Wolf. "Ye can't see my cabin, nuther, frum the tops uv the cliffs uv a cl'ar day onless the smoke gits to gwyin' up straight ez a Injun en blue ez a Yankee overcoat; but yit then the upper eend uv the smoke when it begins to scatter kin be seed; en Scatlett kin cook fur 'em at a quarter a mess."

Penn Grabbé cautiously considered all the surroundings and then put in his sickle while the substitute crop was ripe. During the fall and winter he and his comrades turned many a patriotic penny in support of the sacred cause, reaping where they had sown and sowing in the same place again.

XXI.

THE military prisoners in Louisville were in a constant state of eruption, throwing out men, women and boys for shipment to prisons North or to hot islands South.

Lexie Hallen was arrested on the charge of being a spy, and had no one to intercede for her; General Bright and the Paymentos were with Sherman, and Captain McCook, having been assigned to Sheridan's staff, was witnessing the last of the campaigns in the blood-washed valley of Virginia.

Throughout Kentucky, during that year, patriots were, under secret orders, arrested for their patriotism and humanity and sent as exiles to hostile territory.

This was done in advance of the presidential election, and for the purpose of forcing Lincoln's native State to vote for him; but it aroused public indignation to such a pitch that it well nigh carried the State over to the Confederacy, and subsequently caused it to vote for McClelland by a vast majority.

The Southern authorities were accurately informed of the effect of Jerry Burr's brutality, and sent secret agents to the convention at Chicago which nominated McClelland. Their mission was to note Northern peace sentiments and report back to the Government at Richmond.

Robert Hope was appointed by his Brigade "Delegate at large from Kentucky to the Union-Confederate Convention to be held at Chicago," and instructed, after the manner of trimmers, to vote for McClelland first, Hancock second and Vallandigham third; but if, in his deliberate judgment, Jeff. Davis would be acceptable as the head of the ticket with Mr. Abra'm Lincoln second, he was directed to use all honorable means to secure their nomination. The great grapple of attrition in the wilderness between Grant and Lee and the campaign that took all summer was over when Robert Hope left Atlanta on his dangerous mission. The peace spirit of the North had grown amazingly. McClelland alone was seriously mentioned for the presidency, and by loud acclaim was nominated. The platform on which he stood declared "That after four years of failure to restore the Union by the experiment of war, during which, under the pretense of a military necessity of a war power higher than the Constitution itself has been disregarded in every part! Justice, humanity, liberty and the public welfare demand that immediate efforts be made for a cessation of hostilities with a view to an ultimate convention of all the States; that peace may be restored on the basis of the Federal Union of all the States."

On the reception in Kentucky of the news of McClelland's nomination, the State was thrown into confusion. Jerry Burr was in command, and citizens were shot daily under his orders as alleged traitors, Confederate spies or guerrillas. Women were exiled or imprisoned. He declared that no citizen should sell hogs, cattle or wheat unless "he minded how he voted."

Colonel Taylor Berrien, the brother-in-law of John C. Fremont, and a noble specimen of manhood, had done more to advance the Union cause in Kentucky at the outbreak of the war than any other man. By his introduction and advocacy of mediatorial neutrality, Kentucky was kept in the Union. Thereafter, though high in civil power, he set the example to volunteers by raising a regiment himself, which he led on many a hard fought field; but, desiring peace and union above all else and detesting unconstitutional war methods, he came fresh from the field covered with wounds and began "stumping" the State for "Little Mc."

The election approached. Taylor Berrien was arrested. No one appeared against him. No charge was made or warrant issued, but, in pursuance of a secret order from Jerry Burr, and without warning, he was seized and hurried from the State. The guards left him in the woods afoot, without food, with no change of clothing, in the Confederate lines to meet any fate which might test his stout heart. For McClelland and the declarations of the Chicago platform, one million, eight hundred and eight thousand seven hundred and twenty-five votes were cast the next November. These votes represented twelve million six hundred and sixty-one thousand and seventy-five of the Union population and thousands of soldiers in the field. This mighty nucleus of conservatism was thereafter to be, when the cruel war was over, the bulwark against military government and also the creative and recuperative power which was to restore a union of hearts and rescue constitutional and civil liberty from the passions of its boasted preservers.

Robert Hope and his brother confederates, who played delegates on the floor of the peace convention, fell under the lynx-eyes of Pinkerton's detectives and precipitately fled for Canada. Few of them reached the Queen's dominions, some lost their lives, others were locked in prison, but Robert Hope, after many deflections from the straight road, reached Toronto sick and penniless.

W. W. Cleary, a true Kentuckian and a representative of the Confederacy in Canada, sought him out, and, learning of his mission, furnished him with money and a physician. He lingered all winter with one of war's terrible maladies, and until spring came again was unable to leave his room. When he ventured out hundreds of rumors were rife touching the dissolution of the Confederacy. Soon it became a certainty. But the unhappiness of Canadians over the Confederacy's fall made the final collapse easier to bear by the Americans who belonged within the folds of Lema Sayr's humanity, but who had taken refuge in that cold appendage of British monarchy.

Peace! The cry of Peace! resounded from Appomattox; the North was delirious, the South in mourning! The telegraph flashed the news to city and town. Throughout New England, like silver notes, it rang from valley to mountain, and, sounding its sweet music in the islands of the St. Lawrence, finally nestled its echoes in the cliffs of Quebec. From their heights Robert Hope was gazing toward Massachusetts when he heard the echoes of peace rebound from those foreign rocks to his own country inviting him home.

He looked in the direction of the deep, dark sea, beyond whose waves monarchies ruled and the ancient foes of his country resided. He thought of self-expatriation, but saw his old Kentucky home in the dim distance, standing back in the gathering mists of memory; the common fate of his comrades bade him come; Lema Sayr's smile and the ardor of her eyes blazed in his heart, and a patriotism baptized in blood, greater than sectionalism, freed from passion, extinguishing the stings of defeat and overriding disappointment, cried in his ears, "America is your country!"

At once his purpose was formed, and, when the news of the surrender of the last Confederate army reached Canada he embarked for Boston, hoping to find Lema Sayr on his way home. He had not heard from her since they parted in Shiloh's historic church. No token or keepsake of remembrance had she given him. Only the spiritual face and the gentle voice remained to him, they had become a part of sound and sight; the smoke of battle had not dimmed the one nor the roar of artillery hushed the other. But what might she think of him, now that the cause was lost for which he had fought and bled; now that the songs of Dixie were over and her glory gone on high; now that Kentucky's great son, who led the North, was wrapped in bloody flags of fame and Kentucky's dauntless son, who led the South, was wrapped in a dungeon's darkness? What would she think of him now? was a sore question which he silently put to his heart as he stepped from the ship upon the soil of historic, cultured, heroic Massachusetts.

XXII.

SOME one of that class who, in civil war, wreak vengeance or reap profits had reported the conduct of Lexie Hallen and caused her arrest. This occurred while the campaign in the wilderness was going on, and General Jerry Burr was making merciless war on women, citizens and prisoners in Kentucky.

"Who could have done it?" said Aunt Bina, while shivering in the dull winter light over the scant coals of the kitchen fire. "Who could have been so bad? Poor Lexie is anything but a spy. She couldn't be one. She is too open and sincere. She will help everybody in distress, but never! would she report the condition of others in order that they might be captured or killed. No, no! Lexie wouldn't do that."

"I reckon Miss Lexie wouldn't," said Ned, in a slow, sympathetic drawl. "I'se knowed her long time, en when we user to play togedder when we wus little she wouldn't hurt nobody. She helped me outer de big spring wonce on de ole farm, 'fore we moved to dis ole mean good fur nuthin' town dat don't do nuthin' but put white folks in dat ole pen down yander on Broadway en let ole Jerry Burr do jes ez he please wid ever'body."

"It looks so, Edward," said Aunt Bina, sadly.

She told him to go gather up the trash in the cellar and mend the fire with it.

Lexie's arrest had driven all of the boarders from her aunt's house, and transient people were afraid of being suspected if they stopped there. For several months they had no income and nothing to do. The money they had accumulated by keeping boarders was going fast. They were unable to buy a winter's supply of coal, their credit having fallen with the cruel blow that struck down the spirit of Lexie. Coming want showed its skinny teeth, restless eyes, red with weeping for bread, and its gaunt form. Ned went every day with Aunt Bina to see Lexie, and if the delicacies were not sufficient or good enough, he would, by false pretenses, drop into some bakery by the way and spend his last shinplaster, made at odd jobs shoveling in coal for the neighbors or snow from their steps, for a cake or caramels or a little Shakertown preserves for "poor Miss Lexie." He never let Miss Bina see him slip it under the white cloth that covered what they were taking to the prison. This heart-breaking, spirit-crushing situation lasted for days stretching out into weeks and prolonged itself into months.

Penn Grabbé had not forgiven her for the childish response made to him about asking questions the first time he ever saw her. And when her aunts declined taking him in as a boarder, he let fly the arrow of pique and spite which he had held drawn at Lexie since her unfortunate, but no less deserved, reply.

There was another feeling, too, which had unnoticed grown up in him during the last two years. He did not recognize it, but it made him wish for the power to control Lexie's actions. It was a small thing to get mad at, but, to a keen judge of human nature, Penn Grabbé, in the true sense, seemed to be a small man. He it was who had secretly reported Lexie's part in Robert Hope's escape, of which he learned by eavesdropping during his first stay at her aunts'. After tea, the boarders, Lema Sayr, Lexie and her aunts were in the habit of assembling in the parlor to hear Lexie play the violin, and when the boarders retired the rest would often remain until late in the night to talk with freedom about the interesting or exciting events of the great political war. The latter habit was accidentally discovered one night by Penn Grabbé while entering by the use of the night key which had been given to him because he said, "My business sometimes keeps me out late." As he opened the door he overheard voices which drowned the noise the soft slide of the bolt made with his strong, steady hand. He tipped in like a cat, and, placing his sharp ear to the key-hole of the parlor door, heard, in substance, that Lexie was the chief actor in Robert Hope's escape. Just as he was nestling his ear closer to the key-hole and holding his breath with anxious force, Ned passed, as night watch, along the upper floor. He stooped over the banisters to see what the black bulk at the parlor door meant, and shouted, "Who's dat dar?"

Grabbé jumped like a discovered burglar, and instantly springing up-stairs, as a wolf chased by dogs from the sheep-fold, came to close quarters with Ned, saying softly, "I thought I heard somebody in the parlor."

"De ain't nobody up 'bout dis house sept de wimmin folks, en you a scattlin' in ez sof' ez a cat so nobody heerd ye," responded Ned.

"O I did not want to disturb any one, you know, Ned," said Grabbé in the most considerate tones, and this apparently satisfied him. But he added, "Better keep yo year out a dat key-hole."

Grabbé affected not to hear Ned's last injunction.

Every night after that Grabbé, when he got a chance by Ned's negligence or accumulated duties, would slip down and eavesdrop "the rebels" until he was well acquainted with nearly everything that had happened to them during the war, and much that had happened before. This information helped him to feel justified in causing Lexie's arrest. The aunts were in great distress of mind, for Lexie, as already stated, had been in prison during the dreary winter. Jerry Burr was holding her until Penn Grabbé could collect condemnatory evidence, and also under a promise not to disclose that Grabbé was a "furtherer in the act" of her arrest. He had really never intended to have her tried, but only to punish her and break her spirit. His object was to force her to bend to his will and possible future desires His plan was to take advantage of her condition and place her under lasting obligations for great risks and sacrifices in extricating her from "certain death or endless confinement in prison."

Just when their need was sorest he appeared at their house again asking board, as he often had done before on his trips from Tippling Fork to Louisville "to confer with General Jerry Burr," obtain information or trade permits and gather benefits from anything that might turn up.

Penn Grabbé said, "I always call in order to give your family the chance of my patronage."

He saw they needed patronage and this time pleaded to stay. Ned objected strenuously, "caze nobody doan want dat man 'bout hyar no moah," but the aunts, from stress of need, agreed that he might stay if he could put up with the plain fare."

"O anything will do me; I only want a room, as I have arranged to take my meals elsewhere," he said, "for I hear Miss Lexie is in great trouble and I am going to help her out, if you will never tell on me."

"Thank you, a thousand times, Mr. Grabbé, for your kindness. O! Do help us all you can," dejectedly returned the aunts.

"I will do it, but it will take a little money."

"How much?" cried Aunt Bina, Aunt Julia being then too sick and weak to talk or bear excitement. "We have little, but you can have it all if you will restore our dear Lexie to us."

"You must never get excited; that hadn't ought ever to be done in anything. Keep your wits about you and I'll fetch it around. Let us to business at once. How much have you?"

They scraped together from a little tin box, from a bowl on the top shelf of the cupboard and from the bottom of Lexie's trunk and their own thin, bare pockets the sum of seven dollars and fifty-five cents. He took it and went away.

That night Ned was relied on to get something to eat for them. Ned got it. It was not much. A small loaf of bread and some butter. Coffee grounds were boiled over, and scraps of a diminishing ham furnished forth the supper table. Ned waited on them as usual, but his family pride was cut, and something in his manner was commiserating and roughly tender.

"Missus, it's de bes' I could do ter night," apologetically said Ned. "But Ned'll be hyar wid breckfust in de mornin'!"

The sisters' eyes filled with tears, and the younger drank of the coffee and went immediately and sadly to bed.

Next day Penn Grabbé returned with a sorrowful countenance.

He said, "I have been up all night with General Burr and his officers. They have decided to send Lexie to the Dry Tortugas."

Aunt Julia sank helplessly on the sofa. Aunt Bina remained standing as she listened to the cold, accurate, though manufactured, statement of Penn Grabbé. He dwelt at length on the difficulties he had encountered, the risks he was running and the sacrifices to be made.

"It will take two thousand dollars to save her." Aunt Bina groaned. "But," continued he solemnly, "I have concluded to furnish it myself."

The gratitude of the unhappy women was expressed in beautiful words and with good manners' best effects.

He did not understand this spiritual outgiving of refinement. He thought it resulted from his personal powers, and felt like a man of parts, and thence dragged everything said to him along in the train of his vanity.

"But," said he, "she will be ordered to leave the State, never to return again. The two thousand dollars will only keep her from being sent to the Dry Tortugas. It is too hard, but it was all that I could get General Burr to agree to do, and I guess I did well to do that."

The misery of Aunt Bina had made her dumb, her tongue dry, her eyes tearless and her heart to ache. The poignancy of grief was gone. Its sullen successor, gloomy, terrible and crushing, had taken its place.

"Oh, go and do what you think best!" gasped Aunt Bina.

Plucking up, as it were, "drowned honor by the locks" and manly determination, he said, as sincerely as a heart of leather would allow, "I will have her here by midnight and spirit her out of this wicked city to a safe place."

He handed back the seven dollars and fifty-five cents, saying, "This will do no good; besides, you will need it."

He left the room with a fixed purpose on his brow and success in his firm step. Sure enough, late that night he brought Lexie home.

Her reception must be passed over; it was too touching to mention. She was no longer Lexie in appearance. Pale, fearful, starting at every noise, but drooping and silent when undisturbed by external things.

He had told Jerry Burr how the witness misled him and his own ears deceived him; that it was a case of mistaken identity, curious and misleading, and that the best way out of it was to release her late at night, say nothing about it, and the fear of the future would enable him to have her kindred take her away, so the newspaper reporters could not get the facts of the case and injure the service by disclosing them.

It had not cost him a cent to secure her release, yet he took the note of the Misses Hallen that very night for two thousand dollars, his cupidity banking on the hopes of a posthumous beneficence of a distant relative of whom they had spoken when talking of their chance to raise enough money to pay for Lexie's release.

Grabbé's wife had died two years before, and when he told the aunts of it he tried to cry, but couldn't; that was a thing he could not do. However, they thought he was shedding tears and pitied him in words and looks.

He said, "Because my wife is dead, I will take Lexie to the home of one of the noblest friends I ever had in my life. He is a good and true man, and will conceal her where the minions of Jerry Burr can never find her. You can see her as soon as the rascal thinks she is out of the State and loses interest in pursuing her."

A PATRIOT'S STRATEGY.

"What is his name?" asked Lexie.

"Oh, I am so full of my feelings I forgot to tell. Wolf is his name, my child," answered Penn Grabbé in the conciliatory tones which had so often brought him off victor over those who used grievous words or doubted his sincerity.

Lexie felt religious coals of fire on her head for having misjudged him. She burst into tears, and, wringing her hands, begged his pardon.

"Never mind," said he, "it is more than granted, for I guess at times I do ask too many questions."

Lexie thanked him and looked relieved. The few hours she had been out of prison were brightening the brown eyes; their contraction was slowly turning to expansion; the pale cheeks looked ready to blush and the recuperative power of a pure, courageous, unselfish soul was rapidly reasserting itself. Freedom was working wonders.

Penn Grabbé said, "I guess I'll go to the hotel for the night, so I can better prepare for leaving on the first boat up the river. I had intended going tonight, but no boat leaves till to-morrow. Lexie must let no one see her and she must dress in disguise for our exodus from this city of brick without straw; from this Egyptian darkness."

He was familiar with the Old Testament. When growing up he got the pentateuch by heart, and Solomon, David and Job line upon line. He often drew figures of speech from them and frequently fashioned his thoughts by them, as one can see on looking into his life carefully. When he reached man's estate he rejected the precepts of the Sermon on the Mount because it taught if one cheek were smitten you should turn the other; if a rascal took from you your coat, you should give him your cloak; and if you wished to form a sound judgment about anybody, you were told not to do it. He said he never would teach his children to be beaten, robbed and fooled out of all they made. He admired the business thrift of Solomon which kept him up in the world, although he had such a big family and almost worshiped his capacity for building fine houses with other people's money, timber and labor. David's dexterity in sinning and begging pardon for it had a touch of strategy in it which commanded his respect; and Job's good sense in keeping on the side of the Lord until he got back twice as many oxen, camels, sheep and asses as he lost, was, to his mind, the most thrifty result, in all history, of a fixed purpose. He carried these matured views into practical life and acted in its affairs by the light of human thought as found in the examples of human passions, treating him who loveth all things and trusteth all things as a weakling, a hewer of wood and a drawer of water. Now, for the first time in his life, he had to deal with woman in other senses than courtship for marriage only, and marriage for multiplication, and a wife for drudgery. There was a touch of romance in Lexie's dependence on him; a possibility for love which had never before entered his heart unadulterated with worldly advantage; an opportunity to dig into the mines of his soul for the gold of gallantry and the rich pearls of sentiment. Throughout the night he lay sleepless upon the pillow which seemed hard; no pillow had ever felt hard to his head before.

"What is the matter with me?" he ejaculated; "I feel like paying her way and giving her a better home than Fate Wolf's; but no, there is the place! She can't get away and won't know the war is over, as it is very likely to be soon, until I tell her or cause her to be told."

With a teaspoonful of the leaven of righteousness working slowly in his soul, he arose from the night as tired as Jacob after wrestling with the angel and feeling like love or passion, he scarcely knew which, had had a hip and thigh struggle with cupidity, hypocrisy and strategy.

He ate little and impatiently waited for the hour the steamer should leave. Time hung as heavily upon him as the weights of an honest man's scales and gave him, not measure for measure, but meted out to him a full measure of unhappiness for the grief and misery he had inflicted and entailed on Lexie and her faithful, helpless aunts.

Lexie, muffled in Aunt Bina's dress and bonnet, looking like a modern ancient, stepped aboard the steamer in advance of Penn Grabbé, who carried her light luggage. Aunt Bina stood afar off and watched the breathing boat begin its way up the Ohio.

The bright sun poured its evening rays upon the white hull and curling columns of heavy smoke that rose toward the blue heavens; the west, full of slowly moving clouds, was a conflagration; little white clouds floated away to the eastward ahead of the lessening steamer, making a scene sublimely beautiful.

The view melted away, Lexie was gone, night had come, the night of hearts and the night of nature had joined; Lexie's bosom was full with inconsolable grief; the home was filled with gloom, darkening every nook and corner; the heart of unhappy Ned was full of despair. He cried outright and could not be coaxed to eat anything. "Poor Miss Lexie's gone!" was all that he could choke out of his convulsed throat.

XXIII.

FATE WOLF was bewildered when he saw Penn Grabbé and a young woman coming down the cliff on his "golden stairs." He watched her tremblingly cling at each step to the ladder covered with rushes and knew she must be a stranger. But what absorbed him most was the fine foot that appeared at each timid step downward. Having reached the narrow strip of soil that lay between those rocky jaws which opened as if to swallow the narrow strip of blue sky above them, they looked aloft at the sunlight which shed its luster on the pines and leafless trees standing far above their heads on the opposite heights. From Fate Wolf's cabin the stars could be seen at sundown as at midday from the bottom of a deep well. Lexie walked closer to the side of Penn Grabbé as two brindled dogs, large and ferocious, rushed, barking, from under the western floor of the double cabin.

"You Penn! Hush up, Patter! Begone!" shouted Fate Wolf, and the well-trained brutes instantly obeyed him.

Scatlett Wolf, with her hands under her apron and her pipe in her mouth, came out to receive the stranger woman.

"Howdy, darter; cum in. Take a seat thar in the

corner. Its mighty cold fur sich a weak white-faced leetle gyrl like you to be out, it 'pears to me like," said she, in the kindest, sincerest tones.

Woman understands woman better than man knows man or woman either, and Lexie felt safer from Jerry Burr's bloody rage since she had got so deep down into the earth and found, even there, the law of kindness that inherently belongs to woman.

Before entering, Penn Grabbé called Fate Wolf aside and told him of the great cost and risk to him of Lexie's escape, and how he wished her concealed from all strangers until called from exile or General Sherman could be induced to countermand his cruel order to arrest females. Fate Wolf listened with deep interest. After a pause he asked, "Did Gineral Sherman do that?"

"Had not you heard it? I have got it—here it is," and pulling from his pocket a newspaper, Grabbé read Sherman's order.

"That thar beats ennything ever I seed," said Fate Wolf. "Read it ag'in."

Penn Grabbé read it again literally. It ran thus:

"GEN'L JERRY BURR:
Your military commanders, provosts, marshalls and other agents may arrest males and females, and you may cause them to be collected in Louisville; and when you have enough, say 300 or 400, I will cause them to be sent down the Mississippi, through their guerrilla gauntlet, and by a sailing ship send them to a land" (the Dry Tortugas, where turtles, mosquitoes and yellow fever infest, no green thing grows and water mantles in sluggish brooks and standing ponds) *"where they may take their negroes and make a colony with laws and a future of their own."*

Without comment, Fate Wolf gave a deep sigh and promised to care for Lexie. After a moment's meditation he said: "We do meanness a plenty in gittin' bounty en subter-shoot money fur exerters, but tarnation to my soul—ef I'd a thought enny man—less more a big Gineral—would a dun—sich a thing—en the man what teches that little gyrl will never clim' them cliffs ag'in."

Penn Grabbé, seeing Fate Wolf was in the proper state of mind, handed him the newspaper, saying, "Let her read it, too, and she will be more careful."

"I will," said he, and they went in together.

Grabbé only stayed a moment, then bade Lexie good-bye, telling her not to fear, she was in safe hands, and left for the perilous heights where their horses were hidden. Lexie shuddered as he disappeared in the gathering gloom and could scarcely keep from crying aloud for help. Her heart beat low and weak. She sat spiritlessly watching the red wood coals of fire changing into figures of different animals and people until a stranger feeling came into her lonesome bosom. Fate Wolf went out to the stable—a great rock house in the base of the cliff—to feed Flat-Foot and the cow, while Mrs. Wolf got things ready for supper.

"Kin ye peel 'taters, darter? Scat!" and the cat scampered toward the door.

"Oh, yes," said Lexie.

"Well, when ye git good en warm ye kin peel these fur me," said Mrs. Wolf, placing a pan of potatoes by her side.

Lexie, keen-brained, full of experience, though young, credulous, dejected and uneasy, kept her self-possession and at once made up her mind to please these rough people and make them her friends. She laid aside her wrap and exposed the narrow white lace frill at the base of her beautiful neck. Her luminous brown eyes and white hands, whiter from imprisonment, and her dark lustrous hair and wan cheeks, as she stood full in the fire-light, made Scatlett Wolf cry, "Don't ye tech them dirty taters. I'll wash en bake 'em with the peel on. Jist set right down en git good en warm fur supper—Scat! These blimed cats! ur alys under my feet, en ez fur them brindled dogs, I won't let 'em in a tall."

The last sentence seemed to have been spoken to herself with no one present.

Fate Wolf came in and sat down before the fire, stretching out his hands in front of him to warm.

He said, "Scatlett, it's gittin' cold ag'in. This March weather air blustersome. Little gyrl, do ye hear that wind a risin'? You musn't git skeered tonight, fur it'll play through these cliffs like a bass drum en the old boy a blowin' up his fire fur Gineral Sherman en Jerry Burr. Hev ye seed the 'wimmin order' yit?" handing her the newspaper.

Lexie took it and read it. Her voice trembled and her courage drooped, her eyes filled with tears and Mrs. Wolf came close to her side.

"Don't ye be afeered, hunny. Fate en me ain't much, but we hain't got that low yit."

The March wind howled up the mighty rocky funnel, striking first one of its walls and then the other, sometimes filling a deep rent in the face of the rocks and issuing forth with screams similar to the panther's which once had roamed there, then died away to low moans that made poor Lexie's hair almost rise and subdued all of her faultless courage, which had before been shaken by arrest and humiliation and the awful ordeal through which Kentucky was passing. A thousand anxieties for the fate of her aunts filled her bosom, and when she thought of faithful, honest Ned, ignorant, but loyal to his owners amidst the flow of blood destined to wash away his slavery, and remembered his kindness to her, sick and in prison, her feelings arose in a great volume and overwhelmed her being. Falling on her knees, she uttered a prayer to God that awed Fate Wolf and his wife into respectful silence and filled their souls with the religion of kindness and the first of their sentiments for peace. Fate Wolf had risen to his feet when she dropped on her knees, not knowing what it meant, but when "Thou God of the widow and the orphan, the helpless and the persecuted," fell with anguish, terror and despair from her lips, he bowed his head and Scatlett put her old apron up to her eyes. As the last words, "Help me, dear Jesus," died away and the winds that moaned about the cabin took them and wafted them to heaven, Fate Wolf whispered to his wife and stepped into the other room of the cabin, while she helped Lexie from her knees and into her own bed. After a while he returned and Scatlett said, "Fate, you jes sleep in t'other room ter night. I'll sleep with this yur poor gyrl."

XXIV.

FOR ten weary days Penn Grabbé visited Fate Wolf's cabin, seeking, by pretense and strategy, to find grace with Lexie. She daily wrote letters in pencil to her aunts, trusting them to him to mail. He promised faithfully to see that they were delivered, but, as soon as out of sight, he was reading and destroying them as unconcernedly as he would strip the leaves of spring from a riding switch. Having studied her practical usefulness while machinating to commit her life to his power, he came to doubt her thrift and capacity for housekeeping, the manner of her bringing up being so inconsistent with parsimony or rugged labor, but concluded upon the whole that she might make a good wife. Fate Wolf had shown too much sentiment when referring to General Sherman's order to suit Grabbé's notions, and in this manifestation he foresaw possible obstructions to any violent measures against Lexie that his better judgment might consider necessary. But he dismissed these fears by deducing, from past relations with Fate Wolf, complete subservience to his wishes. Yet recollections of Habbakkuk's pecadillos and Major Paymento's punctilios made him more doubtful of Fate Wolf than he otherwise would have been.

"He never failed me before and I can trust him now in this little matter, as there is no money in it to him from the other side," soliloquized Penn Grabbé as he hurried toward Louisville to learn why no more substitutes would be taken.

Returning as quickly as he had gone, he hastened from home next morning to Fate Wolf's and informed him no more substitutes would be accepted, as the Union had a million and a quarter of men ready for the spring campaign already begun by Grant at Petersburg, while the rebels could only muster one hundred and fifty thousand.

"Well," said Fate Wolf, thoughtfully, "less us look out fur squalls. The thing's agoin' to bust afore the buds bust."

"I believe that is so," rejoined Grabbé, "and I want you to do me a special favor."

"Whatsumever's that?" asked Fate Wolf.

"Do not let Lexie know the war is over, if it stops, until I tell you, or I might get into trouble with the authorities."

"Jist whatsumever air yer reasins fur keepin' peace from Lexie? fur she needs it more'n ennybody ever I seed, ef it cums."

"O well now, my old friend, you must not be too close in your questions. She is a right handsome girl, you know, and my wife's been dead these two years and I need a housekeeper very much."

Fate Wolf, transformed, laughed until the water came into his big, dirty blue eyes, and until the echoes knocked from side to side against the great rocks. Penn Grabbé had his confidence once more, and put a present of dollars in his big, brown, hard hand. As he accepted it he winked at Grabbé a knowing wink, though he knew winking was reprobated by the Bible. He winked, however, because he scented a plot between Grabbé and Lexie, scenting plots being the prominent quality of his half suspicious, half confiding, poorly educated but worldly wise mind.

When they went into the house Grabbé greeted Lexie and told her no letters had come. She suffered intensely, but was meager with her words, taking scant notice of him and his oblique conversation. Fate Wolf saw with a glance that she did not love Grabbé and that aversion marked each guarded gleam of her modest eye. Thenceforward his suspicions became active and his cunning mind alive to the situation. His opinion of plots between them was wiped out. He was satisfied Lexie had nothing to do with any plots about love or marriage.

"Yander cums a nigger down my gold stair steps," cried Fate Wolf, in surprise, as he looked out of his cabin door.

Penn Grabbé had gone into the other end of the cabin, where Mrs. Wolf was weaving on a Daniel Boone loom, for the purpose of pumping her touching Lexie's opinion of himself.

"I haint heerd her speak 'bout ye sense she cum," said Mrs. Wolf. Just at that moment she heard her husband's cry and hurried to him.

All of them rushed into the yard to see the negro

A PATRIOT'S STRATEGY. 187

descending. He was dressed worse than a rag-picker and his black face was still blacker with coal dust.

Ned being in deep disguise, Grabbé did not recognize him and Lexie was barely able to do so. From his manner she caught a warning not to know him. He was such a grotesque sight that it was all Fate Wolf could do to keep the brindled dogs from eating him up.

"What sent the likes uv you hyur? They aint no crows botherin' 'round to be skeered off," said Mrs. Wolf.

"Nuffin much," replied Ned, "but de niggers er all freed en aint got nuthin' to eat en I cum hyar to git sunthin' en work fur Mr. Wolf who's worked fur us niggers all de time ez Mr. Eph Soaks told to me while I wus scatlin' aroun' fur sunthin' to eat up yander in de worl'," pointing toward the tops of the towering walls of rock.

"Ye haint out'n the world yit, yit yer turrible nigh it," said Mrs. Wolf, looking at Lexie, and crying with the next breath "Scat!" to the house cats which had followed them out to see the sight coming down Fate Wolf's "golden stairs." "Cum in though," said she, kindly, "I'll give ye sunthin' to eat. The Good Book says feed the hongry."

Fate Wolf, addressing Grabbé, said, in complimentary tones, "Scatlett ud give old Nick a bite to eat ef he wus to cum hisself," and they went on talking of the unexpected visit while the "wimmin folks" and Ned moved into the cabin.

The middle of April had come, but the latest news

on Tippling Fork was, according to custom, dated in February or March. Ned had carefully listened to the lies Penn Grabbé had told Lexie's aunts the last time he was in Louisville, and intently noted the description of "the safe place" she was in. He could not sleep any of nights after Grabbé had left for thinking of where his poor young mistress might be.

The day following Lee's surrender he left Lexie's aunts to find her and tell her "de war wus over en ole Jerry Burr had run off en to cum along right straight back home."

The morning succeeding the night that Abraham Lincoln, great among great America's great men, was assassinated, Ned descended Fate Wolf's "golden stairs" without knowing that the friend of his race, in the noontide of his glory had gone from earth, flushed with success, yet filling with woe the heart of nations and moistening with tears the cheek of the civilized world.

This national catastrophe, had he then known of it, would not, however, have touched his heart with such sympathy as the sight of 'poor Miss Lexie," whose troubles had caused Ned so many tears and heartaches. He was very humble, but did not, as Uriah Heap, show his humiliation by iteration. He took his place noiselessly on a stool in the dim light of the back part of the cabin, while Mrs. Wolf began to get an early supper.

Penn Grabbé tried to speak to Lexie alone, but she stuck close to Mrs. Wolf, and Fate also kept himself not far away

Finally Grabbé gave up, and, making excuses of which he knew no end, started up the cliff, plotting how he would conquer her aversion and bend her mind to his purpose. From the top of the cliff he stepped into the approaching night beyond, and wrapped himself in its congenial elements, while his thoughts bore a likeness to the darkest hour of the darkest night.

When Fate Wolf went out to feed Flat-Foot and the cow, Ned found an opportunity to say a few words to Lexie during the ins and outs made by Mrs. Wolf getting the evening meal. Lexie began to doubt Grabbé's motives. She wondered if his design were to break her spirit to his spurious affections. Her doubts prepared her for any risks necessary to escape his power, which was secretly coiling around her a destiny far worse than the Dry Tortugas!

Her spirit moaned and all seemed black about her; but courage born of despair came to her heart, and it was filled with hope and high purpose. She reasoned that if he should turn out to have been true, she could be properly grateful and in some way reward him. Just after Grabbé had left, Eph Soaks dropped down with a message to Fate Wolf to meet the boys at Grabbé's house to consider the news of Lee's surrender. Fate Wolf jumped up, went wild over the information and whooped and howled like a wolf, and "hurrayed" for the Union until the silent stars, that twinkled high in the blue strip above his cabin, heard him.

"Will I go?" cried he, repeating Eph Soaks' query.

"You bet I'll go en not cum back ontel I know it's so," and he wildly sang:

'O say kin ye see by the daybreak's early light
The flag uv our countree gleamin' in or out uv sight,
En the star-spangel banner like a trumpet shall wave
Over Tipplin' Fork Crick en the home uv the brave."

"O hush up! Fate, ye air most wild," cried Mrs. Wolf; "go 'long en fetch us back the news."

He mounted Flat-Foot, and, threading his way down Tippling Fork until he emerged from the jaws of the Rocky Gorge, rode as a husband rides for the doctor in the mountains when his wife falls suddenly ill, reaching Penn Grabbé's just as "the dawn's early light" hailed his swift coming.

Lexie lured the brindled dogs, that had become fond of her, to the rock house to milk the cow which Mrs. Wolf had forgotten in the flurries of the evening, and fastened them up. As she returned to the cabin, the soft evening air was still; not a breeze stirred the sounds of the mighty gorge; the stainless stars trembled overhead, and silence, profound, followed the echoes of her voice as it rose in song and died away, pitying and pitiful, for the tones were from heart-strings held tense till almost broken. Ned heard the old familiar voice; it startled him; its buoyancy and gladness, like the soul of music from Tara's halls, had fled, and tears seemed to tremble in every note. She was singing "Home, Sweet Home," that anthem of heaven so dear to the poor man's hearthstone and to the heart of the homeless!

He arose for the first time since he took his seat in the shadows of the corner of the cabin, where, unnoticed, he had remained while Fate Wolf shouted and sang for joy, and slowly and shyly asked, "Caint I help de young mistus?"

"Yes," consented Mrs. Wolf, "go 'long and help her to tote the milk bucket, fur I know it's full, fur the cow haint bean milked this day en she gives lots." Then she abstractedly continued, "I'm tired uv 'em, fur I don't want thim ole subter-shoots en Penn Grabbé cummin' 'bout hyur no more en I hope the blimed ole war is at a eend."

Ned flew through the cabin door as black as Poe's raven to meet and carry Lexie's burden and tell her everything.

Said she, "Ned, we'll leave just after midnight. Mrs. Wolf is tired. She has worked all day, first with me in the garden all the morning ———"

"Did she make you wuck, Miss Lexie?" interjected Ned.

"No, Ned, she is too good and kind to do that. I dropped and covered helianthus seeds and hollyhock in the flower-bed while she planted potatoes, corn and beans in the rest of the garden. The poor old thing has never allowed me to do any work when she could help it. She calls me 'My big gyrl baby,' and says I must live with her always; that she is so lonesome for 'wimmin company,' as she calls it, when 'her man' is gone. I do hate to leave her!"

"But, Miss Lexie, you must go home, fur dat ole Penn Grabbus will kill ye ef he can't git ye no udder way, en awa' up hyar in dis wolfish place he could do it easy en dat ole Wolf wouldn't tell on 'im nudder."

Lexie had no idea of not going; the human heart was but speaking and sympathy only finding relief in the expressions she had just uttered.

"Ned, we go to-night," she whispered, and they stepped in the cabin door, and Ned set the bucket of milk on the puncheon table and softly glided into the back part of the cabin.

At midnight they emerged from the shadow of the cabin together; the stars smiled; the brindled dogs howled in the rock house; Scatlett Wolf, in a dreamless sleep, lay still upon the hard shuck bed, and the God of the weak winged the feet of the deserters; and, as the "golden stairs" of Fate Wolf were mounted, the silver star of freedom stood to the westward over Lexie's home, and, like the wise men of the East, she and Ned journeyed thither.

By daylight they had rambled far through bush and brake, over rock and ravine, and her thin shoes were becoming so torn that the tender flesh of her white feet struck against flint and pricks until the precious blood dyed her stockings and marked their trail.

On the high plateaus of Tippling Fork the streams were then famishing for water. Lexie, faint and thirsting for drink, lagged behind. Finally she could go no longer and sat down on a rock to rest. Ned was crouching on the ground at a respectful distance, awaiting her movement. At length he urged her to go again, saying, "De'll cotch us ef we doan hurry." She arose, staggered and limped along like a poor wounded hare.

He said, "Miss Lexie, lemme help you."

He took her by the arm and stoutly helped her over logs and rough places, parted the bushes for her, and by noon they had reached the ferry at the mouth of Whirling Log creek, where Robert Hope and Sunny Withers, crossing in 1862, met "Colonel" Patter and Fate Wolf. The news of Lee's surrender was spreading like wildfire, and "Colonel" Patter had gone to the ferry and was talking of it with unarmed soldiers. Several citizens crossed while Lexie and Ned rested on the shore. Everybody seemed friendly and the sun shone brighter in old Kentucky's homes than it had for four years.

Lexie's bruised feet had gotten stiff and sore and when she arose to walk to the ferry "Colonel" Patter observed her pitiable condition and at once approached her and said, "My dear madam, I am pained to see you in this forlorn situation. May I have the honor of assisting you into the boat?"

She assented and in a few minutes the boat was shoved across the deep, calm stretch of water which made that part of Blue Lick river not fordable at any time during the year.

When on the other side, "Colonel" Patter said, "Madam, may I ask which way you are bound for?"

Lexie looked at Ned in bewilderment, for she was completely lost and stupefied by fatigue.

He answered, "Lexyunton to git de train."

"So am I," said "Colonel" Patter, "to get the

news. Now," continued he, "lady, if you will accept my horse and can stick on my saddle, you may ride—Long-Leaper is perfectly gentle—and your servant and I will walk along ahead of you."

"O, thank you, sir; thank you, sir. You are too kind. I believe I could not go further, my feet are so sore!"

At once "Colonel" Patter threw the right stirrup leather over the seat of his saddle to the left and turned it into a half side saddle, making the best job possible out of the material at hand. Long-Leaper was led to a stump and Lexie, with "Colonel" Patter's assistance, mounted, while Ned held the horse, and the journey began.

"Colonel" Patter stopped everybody they met and asked the news. Soon the rumor of Lee's surrender was an established fact, but "Colonel" Patter refused to turn back, though she suggested it, saying, "Madam, I may have done many imperfect things, but never yet deserted a woman in distress. My faithful horse is at your service until you are safe and on the train for home."

She and Ned had given him an impressionist's outline of their troubles, but a pretty clear idea of the sickness of one of Lexie's aunts and the growing helplessness of the other, and how she and Ned were so badly needed at home, and how they ought to be there.

"Colonel" Patter, by adroit questioning, discovered that Lexie had no money and Ned only sixty cents of shinplasters left. So he determined to put them through on high points. Like most bloviators, as bloviating results somewhat from idealism, "Colonel" Patter had a tender and romantic spot in his heart, but for courage, moral and physical, he was not greatly noted under exacting demands or in extreme peril.

"At Lexington at last!" said he, after three days' toilsome walking for the sake of woman and Southern courtesy. "Now for the train."

Tickets were bought by him, Lexie's hand was shaken, and, as "Good-bye, God bless you," fell from his lips, the engine whistled—they were off.

The next day he met Fate Wolf and Penn Grabbé at the old Phœnix Hotel in Lexington, a hotel where Santa Anna had slept, where Henry Clay, Dick Menifee, Roger Hanson, Leslie Combs, John C. Breckinridge and Bob Woolly had talked and lounged, and felt bigger for his gallantry to Lexie and Ned without asking their names, "like a Yankee would have done," than any of these celebrities who used to frequent the exclusive little room and fireplace behind the clerk as he stood to face bill-paying guests, or those *non est inventus*.

That little room has heard bright anecdote and pungent wit, dashed with choice bits of public gossip, far into the night many a time, and, had it not been burned, its walls would be odorous with mint juleps as these lines are penned.

But that landmark is gone, with its famous guests, their big discussions, sage remarks and witty sayings; all gone, where to be is equality; but Lexington is no worse for their having been and gone; there was the nucleus of her public thought and there is the revered spot of her best traditions, and there may yet be found her most loving recollections. Would that the old Phœnix and its old guests could rise from their ashes! and may the bright mind of the last of its famed patrons scintillate to the end.

The three patriots of this plain, truthful story went to the bar-room in the Phœnix and drank, first to peace, and second to pensions, leaving off further plagiarism from Light Horse Harry's oration over Washington, who refused a pension for more services than were ever done by any of our million footed pensioners!—or all of them possibly.

XXV.

NEXT MORNING after their return, Lexie was up with the sun. Having put the little cottage in order, she sat down by her Aunt Bina to learn of the troubles which had flown in like a sea upon them during her absence. Poor Aunt Julia had succumbed under the ravages of her old assailant, consumption, and an acute attack of pneumonia resulting from insufficient fuel and cold rooms.

Since Lexie's expulsion from the State, as given out by Penn Grabbé, society had withdrawn, as it so often withdraws from its old friends fallen into financial distress. The sale of their household goods for rent and the surrender of the once popular boarding-house on Brook street were unattended—not even noted—by any of that host of visitors who formerly coined meaningless compliments to their enjoyable entertainments.

They had lived in the obscure little cottage, off in the lonesome suburbs of the city, but three days when Aunt Julia's faithful spirit took its flight from the falling—fallen temple of flesh. Buried in the potter's field, close to the grave of the writer's namesake, who fell under the heavy burden of poverty, Aunt Julia sleeps peacefully, though no flowers bloom above her dust or vain shaft pretentiously points to deeds of transient fame. The house dog was dead; the old purring maltese cat had been lost; the silver plate of ancestors was sold; not an heirloom remained save the portrait of Lexie's father and his fine old violin,

>"The instrument on which he played
>   That was in Cremona's workshop made,
>   By a great master of the past,
>   Ere yet was lost the art divine;
>   Fashioned of maple and of pine,
>   That in Tyrolean forests vast
>   Had rocked and wrestled with the blast.
>
>"Exquisite was it in design,
>   A marvel of the lutist's art,
>   Perfect in each minutest part;
>   And in its hollow chamber thus
>   The maker from whose hand it came
>   Had written his unrivalled name,
>   'Antonius Stradivarius.'"

Lexie listened with moist eyes and a sobbing heart to the history of her unfortunate but once proud and opulent family, now reduced to two descendants—herself and Aunt Bina. Their narrow means had been lessening ever since Robert Hope's escape, for the eyes of spies had then fallen on them and necessitous circumstances were thence made, by gossip and oppression, to enclose them in, so as to cut off supplies and assistance to rebels. Lexie's arrest had capped the climax of their misfortunes, and things had grown from bad to worse ever since, until now the wolf was at the door. It was a bitter day in Lexie's life, but necessity is the mother of invention and sometimes the finder of hidden talents sublime, else why is there a Mary Anderson, or Kentucky's greatest mother and wife, who loveth all things and claimeth not her own; or why was there a Menifee or a Lincoln.

There was no food in the cottage, no fuel, not a ray of cheerfulness, and none with an occupation or with knowledge of an occupation's duties. Ned was ignorant, and possessed only one thing of a high order—a negro's heart in the right place. Lexie, forlorn, arose from Aunt Bina's sad story, which had lasted till the sun hung high in the heavens, and staggered toward the door.

She turned her eyes about over the cottage as if looking at its bare walls, scanty furniture and stinted appearance to gather strength to improve them; her father's portrait caught and held her eyes for a long time, for it seemed to have music in its sweeping graces; withdrawing her gaze, she looked at the time-worn violin and drawing the bow, as she had done in her girlish days, the sounds startled her. The chords of her being were in tune and her distress-bought condition was in harmony with the old violin's heart-consoling music. Again she stroked its sweet strings and new strains came from old pieces she had not played since Lema left them. Her soul was stirred with a new thought which had lain dormant in her nature until accumulated distresses, feelings whose depths the well-conditioned never know, had brought it forth for relief to her weary-laden heart. Thus the chiefest blessings reach mankind through the poor in spirit, they that mourn, the hungry, the meek, the merciful, the pure in heart and the persecuted.

"I'll be a violinist and fill the world, if I can, with music," exclaimed Lexie as Ned entered the door with a loaf of bread, a half dozen of eggs and a pound of sugar he had bought with the remains of the sixty cents of which he told "Colonel" Patter at Lexington.

The sugar was melted, the bread toasted and the eggs boiled. On this they broke their fast.

Lexie was up in arms once more for the battle of life. Soon she was traveling the streets in search of work, but every application was coldly received or rudely repulsed. All that afternoon she walked and begged "her brothers of the earth to give her leave to toil." Thus she struggled until nightfall. The soot and smoke, mingling with its approaching shadows, drove her from her search, and she trudged through the gathering gloom back to their lonely cottage.

Ned had gone forth, too, to take a hand, with Miss Lexie, in the uneven strife for bread and existence, and, long before she got back, returned with the news that he had taken in washing.

A scanty meal sent them to rest hungry. Lexie affected great cheerfulness, and talked hopefully the following morning of what the day would bring forth; but her heart sank heavily and beat slowly, and her faith in humanity began to fail as the last coffee grounds were boiled over for poor Aunt Bina.

With leaden feet she started toward the heart of the great city. While plodding along her weary way, she thought of a ring which Lema Sayr had given her, and the impulse to sell or pledge it for bread-money was almost overpowering, yet she clung to it for memory's sake as a miser clings to gold. As she passed a jeweler's shop her anguish of mind was quite insupportable. She turned back and went in, asked the trinket merchant if he dealt in pawned articles, and, being answered affirmatively, she offered her sacred ring in pledge for a loan. "'Tis ring is quite pritty," said the merchant. "I kint lent you tree tollars unt dat."

Lexie handed it to him. Her heart throbbed with misery and her soul seemed dead as she left the ring in pledge and sought the hard pavement. No work here, no work there, no work anywhere. Night, and no work met again; but by judicious care, with a small part of the priceless three dollars she bought a little food for Aunt Bina and some for poor Ned's hungry mouth. Returning to the cottage she found Ned washing away upon a big pile of clothes of an evidently well-to-do family. When Lexie explained the events of the day Ned laughed, like scared or excited people sometimes laugh, tremblingly, catching his breath shortly at the end, and half shouted, "We ain't a gwine a fail, Miss Lexie."

Seeing how his tones trembled her spirits revived, and she was tempted to laugh as she said, "No, no, Ned; we will work out our salvation with fear and trembling."

Ned resumed his washing and Lexie busied herself with the cooking, and Aunt Bina walked about the cottage in a sprightly manner, saying that she felt better than she had since sister Julia died. She set the table, spreading it over with a white cloth and covering it with dishes saved from the wreck of the boarding-house venture. She and Lexie sat down, with Ned in the background as waiter, and took the first regular meal since their return. After it was over Ned resumed his washing, and by midnight had the clothes ready to hang out to dry. He dropped on a pallet laid in one corner of the little kitchen and fell into an honest sleep before one could count a hundred and slept till the sun rose to dry the clothes. Lexie, with the aid of Aunt Bina, ironed them beautifully, and when Ned delivered them the last of the week his patrons were delighted with his skill and he returned with three dollars and fifty cents, which, like Cæsar's ransoms, did the general coffers of the cottage fill.

"Now, Miss Lexie, you go right 'long back en make dat ole man give up yo ring," said Ned.

Lexie laughed. The stitching began in the cottage before another washing was done, and a little cheerfulness sat at their board once more, sweetening their poverty with its joy-breeding and health giving power. About the third hour of night, while sewing by one of Ned's home-made lamps, Lexie asked, "Why did not some of your old friends come to see you, Aunt Bina, when the officer turned you and Aunt Julia out of the boarding-house?"

The aunt replied, "Ah, child! that is hard to answer. Those of the upper circles of society never like to waste their capacities for pleasure on the sordid hardships of the poor. Many of our old friends were away from the city, besides, our pride would not permit us to ask for help, for in our condition that would have been begging for charity. We thought good fortune might yet turn our way by opening to us some of your father's once extensive property, and preferred to bear our ills silently and hope for something, after all, from that long promising source, though it has so often disappointed us."

Lexie listened intently to her aunt, drinking in every word and enlarging the noble principle of self-dependence in the face of poverty.

"Well, Aunt Bina, you did right, and I will follow your example." Pausing a moment, she added, "I will never ask for charity as long as I can lift a hand or move a foot. I was tempted last week to hunt up some of our friends and ask their aid, but the fear they would think me begging drove the tempter away, and now I feel hopeful because I feel that self-respect and that independence of mind and spirit no beggar can ever feel. One had better die than beg, Aunt Bina!"

"Are you willing, Lexie, to take your place in this kind of life, with its exactions and sacrifices, and wear out your beautiful young days, and when I am decrepit support me out of your slender means?" asked the aunt.

Lexie's eyes filled with tears, and her face that had

been aging under cruel persecutions and grinding poverty flushed with courage and fortitude as she stretched her graceful arms toward heaven and repeated the beautiful constancy of Ruth. Lexie rose, for they could say no more then, and, taking her father's noble old violin from its case, played "Home, Sweet Home," with a pure pathos that sounded like the last wails of the imprisoned soul of this most mysterious of all instruments. She softly laid the violin in its case, and "Be it ever so humble, there is no place like home," fell tremblingly from her lips as she knelt to say her prayers. That night Lexie's pillow was softer, and her dreams came trooping in like angels with noiseless wing, bearing her away from care, trials and woe. She dreamed that failure was better than success, if failure bettered the heart. And the life of the good old violin rose in her sweet visions. There stood her grandfather and his friends who had played upon it; there the Virginia girls whom he had thrilled with its splendid tones, whirled along the ranks of the reel or danced the quick cotillion or the stately minuet; there was her mother listening alone to her father as he beguiled the hours with its powerful depths, its sweet, its delicate tones; all these memories rose in her sleep, until her own exalted emotions, which the sight and touch of the old violin had kindled in this darkest hour of distress, chased her dreams away and she awoke to the realities of poverty, which has few successes, many failures and myriads of trouble. Only one in a hundred rises above its thrall; more are not failures, but all may be happy under its exactions.

XXVI.

WHILE looking at Boston, its old houses, its monuments, its places famous in song, in fable and in history, Robert Hope made incidental inquiry about ancient Massachusetts families. Then he went up to Meadway, and, upon talking with an inn-keeper, learned that the Sayrs descended from Plymouth Rock people, and were living in the old colonial homestead situate near the road Paul Revere took to Lexington to warn his countrymen of the approach of the British.

The next day, as he entered the walk lined with maple trees, he observed on the right of the Sayr homestead, which the inn-keeper had pointed out, a droopy little wing hanging to the main building as if held by unseen hands. It was only one story. The ancient shingled roof seemed to be older than the forest trees of the yard. Odd red lines glowed on each glass of its single window which opened toward Massachusetts Bay. A few steps brought him near enough to read the word "Think" in its brilliant letters, in its Catholic Archbishop's attire. Behind the lower panes of glass he saw a calm face whose composure disconcerted him. The features were blurred by shadows of the walls, and before he could concentrate another look the face had withdrawn, but he had recognized the open countenance. He became strongly excited and with tremulous delight felt the real presence of Lema Sayr. The vision which he had borne in his bosom since they parted condensed at once into flesh and blood. Quicker circulation flushed his face; his steps became unsteady, and when he reached the old hall-door his self-possession almost forsook him. But his steel nerves stood the draft upon them well, and, when the door opened invitingly wide, he was himself again. He presented his card, and the young lady who received him read it with trepidation, shrewdly thinking that this gentleman might be one of her sister's war acquaintances. Inviting him to be seated, she retired with affected composure.

Lema had seen him approach and recognized the manly step and form of the Kentuckian, and was therefore prepared for the meeting. She went into the parlor, where he sat beneath the portraits of her ancestors, and greeted him with modest reserve, but with cordiality. There was no rush or parade or affected laugh which mar the manners of some, or point to slaves of a miserable custom that reduces many a superior woman to a beggar of courtesies and fills many a man with cynicism or the mercenary motives of *post obit* hopes.

The look which had lingered a moment at their parting, the brief grasp of the hand, with its elusive power, its mesmeric force, marked their meeting. Pathetic emotions obstructed their speech and coined into gold the silence that followed. How wonderful a thing is sincerity, or silence, coupled with tact and modesty.

An age seemed to have come and gone since their separation at Shiloh; enough blood had been spilled to float a navy; enough men had been slain to have planted the American flag in Hyde Park, and enough property wasted to pay for every American slave at auction block prices. Yet in a month after the last hostile gun had been fired (and it would be interesting to know what soldier fired it), peace, love and prosperity held out welcoming hands, garlanded with May-day flowers, to all the States then about to be restored to the Union, while secession and slavery, unregretted, lay dead upon the altar of blood.

Bitterness at once died out of a majority of American hearts, dead ashes of the past were scattered to the winds, and the statesman, Charles Sumner, exampling after the philosophy of the ancients, at length moved the Senate to erase from the flag of our reunited country the names of battles which should remind us no longer of the civil war. But the passionate opposed him, the politician roared, and the mercenary pension grabber wrangled like Shylock while demanding his pound of flesh from the bleeding breast of the Republic.

In the light of these events, past and to come, Lema Sayr and Robert Hope sat face to face with wounded hearts, ready for the binding. War's chances and sufferings had inflicted these wounds; birth had severed their peoples; climate and politics had made them Northern and Southern. Could such hearts beat as one? Could love create of such elements a marriage union? Each of them looked inward while silently gazing toward the sea, speaking now and then a few words of health and the weather, that *dernier* resort of conservative conversationalists. At last the language of their hearts burst its chains, and pleasant reminiscences soon made them cheerful. After an hour's talk the field of their adventures was open, and Mrs. Sayr and the sister were called in. He was formally presented. No day in his life had been so full of mystery and music. Propriety marked every word of this New England family, and the exquisite hospitality of women, which makes one prefer to sit at the table of a poor widow than at the feast of a rich man, appealed to the spiritual, and, like one enchanted, he floated with the golden hours, promising to return on the morrow.

The next day was spent roaming through the trees of the yard and jaunting toward Lexington and Concord. The histories of those revolutionary towns were at the ends of Lema's fingers, for she had studied them quite as well as Emerson, whose Historical Discourse in 1835 told of them so scholarly, yet so quaintly. As they returned from the main road into the old gateway that led up to the house, she was all aglow with the excitement of the walk, her blood freely bounding through every vein and artery. Her mind was elastic as her step and her laugh, which always gently trembled as if her spirit were timorous, rippled in low raptures from her throat. She was buoyant, and her humor, which made her tolerant, genial and bright, slowly insinuated itself into every tone and look. Finally she said, "I would like to know if you yet wish to wring the eagle's neck."

"No," said he, "but I should like to pluck one of his fairest feathers."

This scared away her laugh and put a redder rose upon her cheek; and she flew from the advantage given him like the lapwing in alarm from its nest, talking all the while to the best of her disconcerted skill about the battles of Lexington and Concord. He saw, better than a Parthian, where his arrow hit, for it sped straight in front at the selected feather of the eagle. Slowly they ascended the old maple walk, but her waning laughter and her changing cheeks were telling tales and her fast-flowing spirits were beginning to eddy in the viewless mysteries of her frightened heart. As soon as he was seated in the old colonial house, she excused herself for retiring to put off her bonnet and change her fatigue shoes. The sister came in and entertained him while she was gone. She consumed all the time to return that politeness permitted. The subject to which he had alluded lay deep in her heart, but it had lain so long without expression that she tried to believe it was only a fleeting fancy, and that after all it was the mists of memory, and not the murmuring waters of love that filled her soul and gently sang unbodied songs of her Southern experiences. Having poised herself for what might betide, she again entered the room, apparently with that composure which had graced every step and softened each look and word of the morning.

Soon he arose to leave, saying, "I go with some people to visit points of interest in the suburbs of Boston and the Bay to-morrow, but hope to see all of you again before I leave for Kentucky."

Mrs. Sayr, who had come in, said, "May I ask who will compose your party? We may know some of them."

"Oh, yes," said he, "I only know one of them, Major Paymento, whom I met at the Revere House. Through his courtesy I was asked to go along, after he learned I was acquainted with Miss Sayr, 'the great authoress.'"

Mrs. Sayr laughed pleasantly and said, "That is just like Major Paymento. He gets acquainted with everybody, and never tires talking of Lema's skill as a writer."

Robert Hope bade the ladies good-bye with cordial courtesy. Mrs. Sayr detained him a moment to say she would be pleased for him and Major Paymento to dine with them the day after their excursion through the suburbs of Boston. He politely consented to do so with secret pleasure, whose expression, however, he held in check. His soldierly form disappeared, and Lema went to her library to ponder over what she knew of him; to analyze her feelings and relieve her soul of its burden which seemed to be gathering anew as joys and sorrows long since departed forced their painful recollections upon her. Her integrity forbade her to fly from duty for the sake of pleasure, yet her joy and sorrow seemed beyond control, subject alone to chance and circumstance, and alternately to fill her heart with transitory transports or cast her down from perilous heights. She could work, write, serve, but love's caprices and joy's uncertainties played havoc with her feelings and flew away, only to return again with protean shapes to test or destroy by their weird transitions. She had never held, with firm grasp, the rudder of sentiment and steered for port through the sea of human passions. Her sentimental qualities had seemed to float upon the bosom of the waters of life commanding the charity of one, the pity of another, and allowing the subjects of her sympathies to present at will the occasion for their exercise. The fields of her sentiment were determined by chance and time, which appeared to have alternately gleaned until not a sheaf of happy hope was left for this loving Ruth. And now she wondered what she could do if he were to press the conclusions of love upon her and demand the destruction of the reunited ties of home and all the associations which had ripened within the walls of "Think." Her soul had grown deeper, but it was now tumultuous. Here was the publisher's first copy of her first book, named, as one of Tolstoi's, "War and Peace." She took it from its place in the bookcase and read the preface and dedication, dreaming over again the life of the beautiful and courageous characters and touching incidents with which she had graced its pages; there was her "History of Massachusetts," more beautifully written than Dickens' "Child's History of England," which is romance, not history; she took it down and recalled the painstaking accuracy with which she had stated facts and the favor the public had bestowed upon it; and just above the mantelpiece lay, on the "philosophy shelf," her work on the "Science of Life." In it she had written profoundly of the odylic force which Reichenback says burns blue from female finger tips. She wondered if she had been mesmerized by everybody for whom she had had a sympathy. She began to believe much in the overmastering power of exoteric media and intangible forces and in the doctrine that some natures are rarer receptacles of the secrets of nature than others, and that sooner or later all things will be known through that refined electrical apparatus called Brain, which is capable of birth-knowledge of solar time and a thousand overgrown capacities which absorb all the rest; capacities ignorantly called freaks by the unthinking. She spent the whole of the afternoon thinking over the past and trying to quell the strife of her soul. Late at night her mother heard a low moaning and called her, but no answer came. Then she went into the library and said, "Come, daughter, you have sat up too late already."

"O mother! I am so miserable! I must tell you all or my heart will break!" burst from her lips in sad, wild tones of helplessness and despair.

The alert old mother, straight-laced in principle, pure in thought and wise in the laws of nature, sat down by her side, having long since fathomed the depths of Lema's soul, to hear its secrets. Looking into her mother's gentle gaze she read the knowledge which she had just proposed to impart.

"I see you understand it all, mother; I do not want to leave you! but if he sees me again and asks it of me, I do fear my own power to refuse him."

Mrs. Sayr had marked enough of Robert Hope to convince her of his worthiness, and, barring his war record, she thought him an admirable man.

"Well! Well!" said she, "a good sleep will knit up the raveled sleeve of love just as it does any other raveled sleeve. Come! Go to bed and dream of peace and union which has come to your afflicted country and you may find solace for your own afflictions."

Next morning at breakfast Lema was smiling, jesting, laughing, humorous and happy. The sage mother noted it all. For her own good New England heart had made peace through the night with the prejudices of war.

Robert Hope's brave and honorable career chronicled in her mind by Lema's oft-told tales, and his fine form, returning health, chaste speech and spiritual eyes had broken down the middle wall of partition that separated him from the followers of the old flag and enriched her spirit with forgiveness, even with love, for the Union's prodigal son, as she began to consider him. She would not wreck her dutiful daughter's happiness nor mar its future by any grudging withholdings.

The third day like a throbbing Easter came. Lema

went forth for her morning walk, and, as she stood on the gentle slope of the lawn, seeing and hearing the Creator through the insistent forces of nature, her lively imagination, tempered by the chastened feelings of her heart, converted the jeweled dews, the fresh buds, the blooming flowers, the twitter and flight of birds, the sunlit landscape, the blue sky above and the deep blue sea and its deep utterance into human joy—into the purest charms of being and existence. To her the inanimate world was alive, and sea and sky, with their infinite mysteries, were unexplored regions of God's necessary power.

Major Paymento and Robert Hope spent the day with them. War history, war talks, peace, union, the country's future consumed most of the day's conversation. Major Paymento interspersed the last subject with boiling expletives against "the selfish and contemptible patriotism of pension grabbers and pension advocates?" "No soldier," said he, "ought to have a pension except for gallantry on the field, and in that case only for the purpose of elevating the example and causing it to be emulated."

"But what about helpless widows and children of the dead who may have lost their lives in the service, and also those incapacitated by wounds from earning an honest living? All civilized governments have aided such," said Robert Hope.

"That is true," returned the proud old Massachusetts patriot, "but too much should not be given even to these worthy classes, because it tends to reduce soldiers to mercenaries and patriotism to the level of barter and trade, exchanging blood for money and money for blood. Who wants to sell his blood to his own Government, and that a Government of the people, for the people, and by the people? If a man should die for his home, his wife and his children without being moved to it by filthy lucre, he certainly should be willing to be killed and wounded like an American and not like a Hessian who fights alone for pay and plunder. I detest mercenaries of any country, and *do* hope that the American Congress will *never* reduce the dead and wounded soldiers of the Union to the level of bounty jumpers, pension grabbers, service pensioners and dependent kin, their uncles, their cousins and their aunts, by placing them on the same rolls together. Sir, rather than be such a mendicant, I would prefer to share the military glory of the rebels who fought like lions without either pay, provisions or pensions, losing all they had and then refusing to complain of their hard luck."

Every word the old Major uttered was emphasized with vigor, with great earnestness mixed with royal contempt. Seeing that the conversation was too realistic, Robert Hope artfully turned its current and soon the social geniality of the old patriot straightened out the kinks and wrinkles of his mind into which the thought of unworthy pensioners had crumpled it.

"I read," said he, "Miss Sayr, your last work with great interest. It is a peculiar view of life. I had never before placed the forces of life in the category of the exact sciences, and, while you treat the subject with skill, I must say I thought you wrote from experience as much as from theory or logical concepts."

Lema blushed violently because Major Paymento's remarks struck the keynote of her life which formed the foundation stone of her book; and what if he knew of the vicissitudes of her feeling heart, and should branch off into particulars. He was just honest enough to do so. This thought frightened her until the roses of her cheeks withered into snow. Her color gradually returned while all seemed to be thinking only of the ideas Major Paymento was advancing respecting her latest and most successful work.

Major Paymento continued the thread of his thoughts and descanted most learnedly and politely upon the intrinsic merits of "The Science of Life." After exposition of various theories and expansion of those contained in her now famous book, the table talk descended from its philosophical perch and spread its wings of wit, fancy and mirth over all who sat around this social board.

Major Paymento said, "I have pulled the bridle off my tongue and let it run too much; but who could obey the Scriptures when pension leeches and the whole problem of life confronted him at once?"

All declared that he needed no excuse, and Robert Hope said, "Refreshing candor and disinterested patriotism will never tax the temper of an American dinner party."

"Gracefully said, sir!" cried Mrs. Sayr, and the company, like the committee of the whole in the House of Commons, rose and reported progress to themselves and sat again. After an hour's pleasant conversation they resolved to meet at another time, if opportunity should ever offer itself, and Robert Hope and Major Paymento departed.

Lema went quickly to her study, threw herself into the old maple chair, and, folding her arms in a sad knot upon the writing table, sank her face deep in the loose silken sleeves of her gown.

"What! gone without a word?" she sadly repeated. After studying with closed eyes this quotation, she arose, and, looking through the window and far away where the moaning breakers roar, tenderly repeated for comfort the other two:

"Ay, so true love should do: it cannot speak;
For truth hath better deeds than words to grace it."

The next day he came again, and they met in the consecrated library; there alone their words were spoken; there their souls, with full tender communings, made the very walls feel happy; there they lingered till the fires of everyday life seemed burnt out and all else ignoble, commonplace. In the light that streamed through the red-lettered window, surrounded by the books of her choice and of her making, and where the unrest and roar of the sea were ceaseless, they bound up the wounds of their hearts made one by war's chances and sufferings. He went away with the sweetest and richest treasure of earth, a pure woman's plighted troth, and eagerly sought his old Kentucky home, nestling beneath the vernal sun of a balmy climate, and in the bluegrass and bursting flowers of a generous soil.

His old father tottered to the door, the mother and sisters ran to the gate, Aunt Usley stood with her hands on her hips in the yard, and the sunlight of day welcomed him back to the hearthstone, whence at midnight he had fled, nearly three years before, a skulking outcast with a homesick heart.

After shaking hands with him, Aunt Usley went waddling back to her cabin, muttering, in mild indignation, "Aunt Usley wa'n't gwine to tell dem ole Yankees on Mos Robert, en she didn't, nudder."

During the first week of his return he had outlined and illustrated his whole essential career as a soldier, and had also confided to his sisters and mother something more absorbingly interesting than stories of the war. When the father learned—which was as soon as the mother got an opportunity to tell him—of Robert's engagement to Miss Sayr, he declared the wedding should not be deferred a day beyond what was necessary for Robert to get ready and return to Boston. All joined in a letter to Lema's mother, and Robert wrote many details bearing on their immediate and ultimate future, adding some very strong reasons in favor of his father's views. After a fortnight's consideration the two families were at one, and in the leafy month of June Robert and Lema stood upon his father's wide veranda, the recipients of the graceful courtesy and love of his sisters and the adoration of his father and mother.

The flowers and fields were brilliant; the quail were whistling, "Bob White," on the fences; the free black man and the slave mule were lazily "plowin' de coan," as of yore; the mocking bird's song was more nearly human than ever, and once more the sun shone bright in this old Kentucky home.

All hearts were joyous and gay over Lema's advent into the family, for Robert, and Robert's word was to be trusted, had said her heart was good and kind, her mind both solid and brilliant, and her life blameless. Profert had been made by him of her beauty on dull canvas, but the mother declared, and the sisters, as soon as they saw her, reiterated, that it had fallen far short of the truth.

The old father led them into the great wide hall, on either side of which hung the family pictures and the portraits of favorite Kentuckians—Henry Clay and Richard H. Menifee, for this was an old Whig family, Albert Sydney Johnston and John C. Breckinridge—brought from their hiding places when peace was made, because there were no Southern soldiers left to make war, and looked intently, softly, into their eyes while holding each by the hand and said, "Robert, this looks like the cruel war is over and a perfect union between North and South established." The mother wanted to take things a bit seriously, but the daughters laughed with their cheeks, with their eyes, their hands and feet, their joy was unconfined and knew no bounds.

Preparations for the wedding guests were in a high state, with no ancient mariner about. Colored boys, mounted on thoroughbred horses, had scurried along the pikes and over the blue pastures for miles around delivering the invitations.

The reception, in those days called an infair, began at eight o'clock that evening. The house was filled with bluegrass beauties, those of the very white foreheads, chestnut brown hair, which predominates in the bluegrass region, brown eyes and blue, fine forms, all graceful, with not a waist like a wasp's, but *a capite ad calcem*, a finished natural production, a production which springs from a soil based on limestone resting solidly under red adhesive clay, which supports the deep dark loam that carpets the earth with unique grasses. The men, from whom Frederick the Great and Napoleon would have given a province to pick an old guard or cavalry corps, were there—the analogy and precedent from which gods might have sprung, and, by any test of excellence as a body, the best physical growth of human beings in the republic—perhaps on earth.

Music and flowers and dancing, bright humor, courtesy born of courage, minds benefited by, but, unlike those of Boston, not wholly made up of culture, good, graceful intercourse, free from heavy philosophy, unbookish, but gallant and intelligent, such as killed care and made the occasion pleasant and happy, squeezed from life its acrids, its war-born passions, its bloody memories, and crowned the marriage of Robert Hope and Lema Sayr with an old Kentucky welcome.

When the feast, such as Greek gods never tasted,

was announced, the table was a poem and the grace of the people more graceful than the table and better than the dinner.

Lema Sayr Hope was the object of the daintiest and manliest courtesies, and her perfect grace in movement, clear blue eye, high-purposed countenance, gentle voice and rare laugh made all around her smile. Though everybody danced well, yet she was the poetry of motion and a whirling song.

General Bright had been invited and was present. He said, "Everything would be complete if poor little Lexie were here." At the table and during the intervals of the dance he received marked attention, for he was native to Woodford County and to the manner born. He had graduated from the Frankfort Military Institute and entered the United States Army before the war. During the great struggle he rose rapidly from Lieutenant to Colonel, from Colonel to Brigadier General, and near its close received the double brevet of Major General of the Regular Army and also of Volunteers for gallant and meritorious conduct on the field. Every son and daughter of Woodford, nine-tenths of whom were Southern, claimed a joint right to his fame, and he was consequently very popular at Robert Hope's wedding reception.

Major Paymento and Mrs. Paymento had accompanied the wedding party from Boston. The old Major fraternized beautifully with the Kentuckians, but the subject of pensions being mentioned, he broke forth into reprobating pensioners until he lost his listeners. Mrs. Paymento was expostulating with him when Captain McCook joined them.

"Captain McCook," said she, "my husband is so opposed to the extension of pensions that he has got so he loses his temper whenever the subject is mentioned. *Now do you* think that *is* right? Ought not patriotism to be rewarded?"

"No," interrupted the Major, "for old Sam Johnson said patriotism is the last refuge of scoundrels who want a reward for it, and I am beginning to believe him."

"That man is little to be envied," said Captain McCook, "whose patriotism would not gather more force without a pension than with it."

"That is the law and the gospel on the subject," exclaimed the Major, who, at that moment, caught General Bright's eye as he approached them.

"What do you say about pensions, General?"

"I never thought of one and know nothing about the subject."

"Now, there is disinterested patriotism," cried the old Major, "go through the war, be wounded three times and brevetted six times without ever thinking of a pension."

"Come, come," cried Mrs. Paymento, "you must stop this pension talk. Captain McCook, do you intend to remain a bachelor and do without a pension too?"

"I do," said he, "for Miss Lema Sayr has joined the rebels and I won't join the pensioners."

All of them laughed, for this was cheerfully said by Captain McCook.

"But here comes some Woodford beauties who will change your mind," cried Mrs. Paymento, and Captain McCook immediately secured one of them for a waltz and the next set, leaving General Bright and Mrs. Paymento deeply engaged in conversation with Mr. and Mrs. Robert Hope, while Major Paymento was holding his peace on pensions.

The writer leaves them under the lovely form of the bow of peace in the full pursuit of happiness under the Constitution of the restored Union, crying, as St. Paul Sarpe cried in Venice, *"Esto Perpetua."*

He who reads this allegory and does not feel that this is a Union of hearts with one patriotism, one humanity, holding high the torch of Liberty that will yet enlighten the world, is unfit to enjoy the civic rights of an American.

XXVII.

THE armed War of Politics was over, but with tongues it was yet to last for decades to come. The occupation of contractors, sutlers, bounty jumpers, war-shirks and substitutes was gone, but pension possibilities had a new birth and soon began its trespassing acquisition of a limitless lease upon the property and earnings of the American people.

At the following election Fate Wolf stood for Magistrate of the Tippling Fork precinct, on the platform, "Let us have Peace, Plenty and Pensions," which Penn Grabbé had, with "apt alliteration's artful aid," constructed for him. The election was very exciting, but, when the polls closed and the old Union hero left for Roan, he was three to one ahead of his opponent. Late in the evening, as he rode into that patriotic town, he sat Flat-Foot with original dignity—modified, it must be said, with some swagger. He had a right to be proud, for he had led the ticket and crushed the opposition.

Some one observed his approach and shouted, "Yonder comes Fate Wolf!"

Immediately Eph Soaks, Tom McShite, Lyt Wardrip, "Colonel" Patter and twenty others came rushing to meet him, cheering him as he came.

Dismounting with unequivocal strength and the manner of men loaded with pride, he cried, "Hyur, boys, one uv you hold Flat-Foot. I'm turrible tir'd, fur I've bean a runnin' ever sence mornin' like a skeered fox houn'."

At that epigrammatic condensation of results his admirers made the welkin ring. Instantly he was seized by a half dozen and hoisted to their shoulders and carried into the bar-room. There he ordered the drinks for the crowd upon the same bar-counter on which "Colonel" Patter, in 1861, laid off the battlefield of Bull Run.

Eph Soaks said, "When I left the Tipplin' Fork at dinner time Fate Wolf wus a out-runnin' his namesake," covertly alluding to a wolf.

Tom McShite sniffed and whisked about the bar-room, repeating, "En he kep' on a out-runnin' 'em."

This brought out a loud laugh from old Jo Soaks, who had followed them into the bar-room.

Penn Grabbé, raising his glass to drink a toast to Fate Wolf, peace, plenty and pensions, said, "I propose to give 'Squire Wolf an office in my Hallen house free of rent during his whole term and all my pension business besides."

This statement was loudly applauded, but Fate Wolf took it very much as a matter of course, "fur," said he, in response to the toast, "I made the fight on his P. P. P.'s en never crossed a 't' nur blacked a 'i' en ez a matter uv jestice I except his properzition."

This response produced a diminutive riot, which

lasted full five minutes. Just then several of the Hawkins, Fadges, Blacks, Whites, Greens, and Browns, Smiths and Jones arrived from Tippling Fork in great triumph. It was then growing dark, but Roan, and especially Pension Grabb street, was ablaze with the victory of the old Union hero. Penn Grabbé, having seen that the boys were properly fraternizing on Fate Wolf's platform, quietly withdrew and left for home. Along the way his thoughts took a skillful turn and with the keenest mental strategy he traced the lines of future plans. He was already a pension attorney and had learned the clandestine details of that position with an accuracy which poor Chief Justice Long, whose total disability curtailed his earning power to a meagre six thousand a year, afterwards might have admired extravagantly. A bright political future seemed to open before Penn Grabbé and every day thereafter to widen his plans and free his conscience from little shackles. He had cast his horoscope over the future and felt he was master of its destinies. His perfected plans only remained to be executed.

Fate Wolf, having received his commission, took the official oath and entered upon the discharge of his duties. He established his main office in his double cabin in the lone obscurities of Tippling Fork and opened a branch with Penn Grabbé in the Hallen house. The latter explained to Fate Wolf that it was necessary to have a large number of blank forms on hand on account of anticipated flush times in pensions. He showed him the forms adopted by the Pension

Department, and that almost everything was alike in each claimant's case, leaving but little to be filled in with original matter.

'Squire Wolf said, "It would be a big savin' uv time to hav sich forms a lyin' aroun'."

Penn Grabbé also suggested that it would be a great convenience to pension patriots to have the forms sworn to in advance, so they could be filled up thereafter as facts developed without calling any Cincinnatus from his plough too often.

This suggestion struck a vibratory chord in Fate Wolf's nature, a chord which gave out a response at once loud and harmonious. He started home that night, as was his wont after office hours, and, in deep revery, rode the whole way. He conceived a lofty respect for the technical ability of Penn Grabbé, and considered him the most dexterous-minded man he had ever seen. It is true, he had some misgivings of the future, and felt a little like Quirk in the hands of Oily Gammon, but expressed his fears differently, often saying to himself, "I reckon he wouldn't play Ben Dick Arnold on me ef them loaded forms mightn't shoot straight or wus to bust in our hands."

He talked it all over with Scatlett that night, and she said, "Don't you do nary wrong thing fur nobody nur fur nothin', nur Penn Grabbé, nuther."

He said he wouldn't "onless by refusin' it mout cheat a honest patriot out'n uv a jest pension."

Before many days had come and gone, Eph Soaks applied for a pension. A difficulty, in the barbarous language of lawyers, arose *in limine*. He never had been enlisted in any regiment by the name of Eph Soaks. The name under which he had enlisted stood on the rolls opposite the word, "Deserter." Epaminodas Brown, called Ep for short, had gone with the army from Tippling Fork. He had neither heirs nor kindred, and had heart disease. While his name was on the muster rolls, he merely followed the camp to see if he could stand it. Nobody on Tippling Fork believed, when he left, that he could live through the war. At Big Hill an unexpected rebel yell, coming, as it did, from toward the rear, untimely frightened him to the viewless shades or until his heart stopped beating, which was the same thing.

As Eph Soaks had done a great deal of service and had nothing much to show for it, it was concluded that he might be a kinsman of Ep Brown, and, being equitably entitled to a pension, Grabbé thought there was no harm in Eph Soaks adopting the name of Brown. In due time the pension was obtained with large arrears, and natural Eph Soaks, but legal Ep Brown, was restored to his old-time prosperity.

Penn Grabbé had obtained access to the muster rolls at Frankfort and had in his employ at Washington an agent who kept him informed of the contents of the rolls in the War Department. By these means he discovered many curious records of the life and services of the soldiers of the Union.

One day, while waiting for a pension client, Penn Grabbé said to Fate Wolf, "I believe God was on the side of the Union soldiers from Kentucky and against her rebels more than any other State."

"Whatsumever makes sich a belief ez that in ye," asked Fate Wolf.

"Well," said Penn Grabbé, "Kentucky had seventy-two thousand, two hundred and seventy-five Union soldiers and only two thousand, three hundred and twenty-five were killed and died of wounds—one out of thirty-one. The rebels had twenty-six thousand, two hundred and forty-nine from Kentucky and lost one thousand, seven hundred and forty-eight out of five thousand at the battle of Stone River, and more than one-third of the whole number during the war."

"Whew! What a pensionabler crowd them rebels would a made hed they bean on the right side," regretfully cried Fate Wolf.

"You just wait," said Penn Grabbé, "until this pension fight gets warm and all our Union kin become interested then you will see Kentucky with thirty thousand pensioners, and a good chance for forty thousand."

Penn Grabbé was a prophet, without honor at that time, except with pension applicants, but he lived to see the day when wrapt Isaiah's prophetic fire was not more bright.

"Here is another providential thing I have found out from the records," remarked Grabbé. "Kentucky had twenty-two whole regiments on the Union side that went through the war and never got an officer killed, and two regiments in which not an officer or man was killed or wounded, and her corps of engineers was equally fortunate."

"Well, that beats ennything ever I seed," said Fate

Wolf. "Ef ever a fair gives premiums fur soldiers what cum out the best in this yer war, Kaintucky will take the blue ribbon, ur a white feather, one ur tother."

"I must tell you of a curious incident while we are talking of the marvelous," said Grabbé, apparently not noticing Fate Wolf's satire. "It occurred at the battle of Big Hill. Eph Soaks was there with us, you recollect."

"I reckon I do reckerlect onless my reckerlect run off like we did," broke in Fate Wolf with a big laugh while his big, dirty blue eyes filled with tears.

"The day before that disaster Eph Soaks became acquainted with Colonel Calfe," continued Grabbé, "by presenting to him a canteen of milk and a jar of honey, which, among other things, he had captured from a rebel citizen who lived in that land of milk and honey a half mile from the turnpike on which we marched to meet Kirby Smith. As the flight began from Big Hill, Colonel Calfe thought he saw Eph Soaks run against a tree and kill himself. But the Colonel was mistaken. Eph Soaks had only been Absalomized without the fate of that rebellious prince. From the entanglements of limbs and grape vines into which he had run, he escaped with scratches and bruises, while the jest of those that never felt a wound, will make good pension evidence."

The reader will remember it was suggested in the early pages of this history that after the battle of Big Hill the next roll call of the Flying Seventh cavalry was made in the State of Ohio. Eph Soaks was missing and Colonel Calfe reported him killed on the battlefield and at once had his name placed upon the rolls of Company C, as he intended doing before the battle began. Thus his name appeared on the army roll and the most honorable of all discharges was attached to it, "Killed in battle."

When Penn Grabbé discovered these facts and found the name of Eph Soaks on the rolls, he was delighted and at once filled up a declaration for Eph Soaks' widow, who signed and swore to it before 'Squire Wolf. It stated that E. Soaks was enrolled in August, 1862, Company C, Seventh regiment of Kentucky cavalry, usually called "The Flying Cavalry," and was killed in the battle of Big Hill, leaving a widow and seven children to mourn his loss. The proper affidavits of identity and correspondence to the deceased were made and Eph Soaks, officially dead, though corporeally living, got another pension for his widow and children with whom he lived to enjoy it for many a good day thereafter.

This instance modifies the charge that "Republics are ungrateful."

He never wavered in his politics but once and that was when his claim for a pension on account of wounds received in battle was rejected. He then took a solemn oath that if ever Republican officials rejected another claim of his he would vote the Democratic ticket, and if another war broke out they might do their own fighting, for he wouldn't fight another lick.

Fate Wolf said, "Eph Soaks would make wun uv the best sperrit mejjums in the world, fur he is still alivin' en hez bean dead twice."

Many and many were the doubtful and difficult but patriotic claims for pensions which Penn Grabbé's strategy successfully established. His fame soon went abroad over all the land as the best pension attorney practicing at the pension bar. Claimants with flaws of all sorts in their claims flocked to his office. He had increased his reputation very much by giving it out in speeches that he only wanted to know one thing to get a pension and that was, "Is the claimant a patriot." In such cases he was never known to fail until his strategy was foiled in an attempt to rerate for total disability the pension of Chief Justice Long, of Michigan, who, dependent upon himself alone for a livelihood, was making only six thousand dollars a year as Judge of the Supreme Court of the Lake State!

That failure hurt Penn Grabbé's reputation because it was said by Fate Wolf to be one of the most deserving pensions ever demanded from the Republic.

If Chief Justice Long had lived in Kentucky when this unexampled ingratitude was shown him by the Government it would have turned the thoughts of Kentucky's thirty thousand pensioners to the tolerable conditions which successful treason might have established. Even "Colonel" Patter, who came near being led away into rebellion, remembered him from a casual loan in early life and named his celebrated piebald stallion, Long-Leaper, in his honor, thus illustrating, in marked contrast, the difference between individual and governmental gratitude.

Penn Grabbé ultimately became very popular and through sheer pressure of his clientel was forced to run for Congress.

While absent on his canvass, Fate Wolf, mousing among his papers one day, found the title deed to the Hallen house. He read it carefully and with great interest, thinking possibly that Lexie Hallen might be "kin" to its original owner. He had formed a great attachment for her, always regretting her flight from his double-cabin. Like most men of his section, he had an innate respect for a woman and would rather fly to her assistance than take sides against her on any pretext. But these tendencies might be overcome, especially in one like Fate Wolf, whose cupidity made such a slave of his better qualities as to cause him to obey or trust the vilest of men. There seemed to be flaws in the deed, and he applied to the County Clerk for information. It appeared that the Hallen house and six acres of ground had escheated to the State "without office found" many years before the war, but was afterwards disescheated and sold for taxes, Penn Grabbé becoming the purchaser at four dollars and eighty cents. The deed from the sheriff showed on its face that no advertisement of the sale for taxes had preceded that confiscatory act, and that it had been made by one of Penn Grabbé's own deputies while he was sheriff of Branch county before the war.

Fate Wolf immediately wrote a confidential letter

to Lexie Hallen explaining at great length and much technical confusion the condition of the title, winding up by saying, "Ef ye air akin to Richard Hallen I kin git a good house en six acre uv ground back fur ye. Cum right on without enny failure whatsomever to Roan. The old umin will be turrible proud to see ye ennyhow. When ye git hyur say nuthin' to nobody but me en I'll do ye right, hunney."

For years Penn Grabbé had given himself no thought about the title to the Hallen house. His claim had ripened by lapse of time, under color of title, into public belief, and long since, like his conscience, his title seemed to have been quieted. In fact, he had improved the house at considerable expense before opening his pension office in it. These improvements added much to the beauty of Pension Grabb street and Bounty Jumpers' avenue, which crossed the former west of the Hallen house. He had planted rose bushes, water maples, chestnuts and evergreen pines in such profusion as to attract the attention of visitors to Roan. He said he cared little about such things, but the prosperity of the town and the good of his neighbors induced him to make the improvements.

On his return from his first electioneering tour he reported the people enthusiastic for him. Fate Wolf said nothing about the discovery he had made of the title deed. Pension claimants were pouring in more than ever, and the demand on Penn Grabbé's time was interfering with his race and rendering Fate Wolf uneasy lest Lexie Hallen might come before

A PATRIOT'S STRATEGY.

Penn Grabbé again went out upon his canvass. Hence Fate Wolf mislaid some of the most difficult claims and so manipulated the office as to reduce pressing business and render Grabbé's presence no longer necessary.

"Now," said Fate Wolf, "is yer time to make this hyur canvass beat ennything ennybody ever seed afore it. Ye see ef ye git to Congruss the patriots will git the pensions, en ye kin hev 'em encreased ontell every man what toted a gun endurin' uv the war will tote a pension; en there's yit more I'll say, thur present famblies ort to have some pensions fur ever' wun uv 'em frum father to mother, sister to brother and uncle to cousins whethersomever they be in tens or dozens. You ort to jist advicate that the oldest grandson en the youngest son ort to be made a prime uv gennitur patriot by givin' 'em a pension fur life en their fust airs fur ever, so that the Government kin alays hev soldiers fur force wars comin' off yander in the future."

Penn Grabbé said, "I am willing to advocate these views, but the time is not ripe for sweeping justice to be done patriots of our civil war, but it will come, and when it does pensions will make more patriots than any other one thing that has ever been tried in the history of governments."

The next day he started upon his canvass and left Fate Wolf in charge of the office, hoping that Lexie would come before Penn Grabbé got back.

XXVIII.

LEXIE received Fate Wolf's letter just in time to revive declining hopes which were rapidly sinking under the unappeasable demands for rent by the owner of the cottage in which they lived. It was eight dollars a month. They were too poor to pay it. Each week they either fell behind or went hungry. She had tried to get violin students, but failed because her bowing was so carelessly easy to mothers ignorant of the poetry of motion or bent on nothing less than Ole Bull himself for a teacher.

Their landlord said, "This is the last notice I intend to give you. You must vacate to-day, but you've got to leave that big picture on the wall. I want some security for my rent that'll be due me, after the sale of your table and cooking stove. They won't bring much."

It was the portrait of Lexie's father the landlord coveted.

"If you let us have it," begged Lexie, "you may take our dishes, knives and forks, some of them are silver, here are three silver spoons and two dessert spoons and the silver ladle."

"What is the picture worth?" asked the shrewd landlord.

"How much is the picture worth? Why, sir, it is one of Jouett's—Kentucky's noblest artist! It cost eight hundred dollars, so mother told me many a time before she died."

He thought for a moment and said, in a trading tone, "Your things won't bring anything at public sale, and to save myself I must keep the picture."

Lexie's pride sank, and, with a troubled heart, she went slowly away, casting her last trembling glance on the picture of her father that hung upon the little cottage wall. Thus passed from his family the picture of him who, once wrote for Kentucky's highest tribunal the language of law with such clearness, force and elegance as to command the respect of Westminster Hall, within whose ancient walls his opinions are yet cited as sound principle and wise precedent. They parted with the heirloom and started for Roan. Ned went by Mrs. Morningstar's and collected three dollars and fifty cents for the last washing and ironing. In the hurry Lexie had forgot the dear old violin and ran back to get it, but the landlord, having found it on the premises, claimed it under distress law as a sort of rack rent, which amounts, according to Blackstone, to the value of the premises rented. In this instance the violin was worth more than the cottage. Fortunately, however, the landlord, being non-musical, was ignorant of the value of "old fiddles." He said, "I hate their noise, and you may take it along for a dollar or two." Lexie had one dollar and eighty-five cents. Like generous-born people, who never learn the cunning which belongs to money-holding, she frankly told him what she had.

"I would," said she, pleadingly, "give you a hundred times this amount, if I had it, for my dear, dear old violin!"

"But you will never have it. You can take the old rattle-trap for the dollar and eighty-five cents."

She gave him the money; it was all she had. He handed her the old violin, trembling then to speak its silent notes of woe which were yet to move the hearts of men to love the poor, the lowly brave, the world-tired victims of hard circumstances.

She hugged and kissed it, and, placing it in its case, fled the presence of the landlord. Rejoining Ned and Aunt Bina, the journey to Roan began. It was late in the afternoon.

She said to her despondent aunt, "We can do no more by staying in Louisville and no worse by leaving it, and may recover some of my father's property and yet have a shelter from the storm."

They took the road toward Perryville, walking slowly along until nightfall. They called at a farmhouse which Lexie recognized. She said to the farmer, "We wish to stay over night."

"Certainly; come in!" was the prompt response that drowned Lexie's concluding statement that they had but little money to pay.

He was a well-to-do farmer, a fair type of Kentucky's best. Ned was sent to the kitchen where slaves once inhabited. Negroes were still there, though slavery was gone. But the farmer fed them just as well as ever and they seemed to work better, the vicious having gone to the slums of the city or into the slavery of subordinate politics. Liberty had done the sifting.

Lexie and Aunt Bina were seated in the family room until a chamber could be prepared to receive them. "Come," said the farmer's wife, "your room is ready."

When supper was announced, Lexie and Aunt Bina, refreshed, descended the stairs, and, taking seats at the table, heard this odd blessing, "God bless everything and everybody."

The farmer was not a talkative man and his wife was sparing with her words, yet they always said enough and at the right time.

During the meal not an inquisitive question was asked, nor a questioning look passed between the farmer and his wife. Embarrassment was banished by discretion and courteous attention to the wants of Lexie and Aunt Bina.

After they finished eating, the farmer's wife said, "You have eaten nothing scarcely, but I hope you are well and will make it up at breakfast after a good night's sleep."

"Thank you," said Lexie, "we have had a delightful repast, and I am sure we can sleep soundly under your roof."

"Indeed, you can if welcome makes sleep," said the farmer.

Lexie and Aunt Bina chorused, "Thank you, sir!"

When the farmer placed under the piano their

bundles, that appeared to belong to persons once well-to-do or the educated poor, he had 'spied the violin case, which, by his wife's direction, Ned had laid on the piano.

After supper when conversation began to flag he asked, "Who is it plays upon your instrument? I should like to hear some music?"

"Yes," said his wife, "Mr. Mims dearly loves music. Please play for him."

Lexie arose. He handed her the violin, looking straight and searchingly into her face, but did not recognize her. He apologized for looking at her so, saying, "I really thought I knew you or had seen you somewhere."

Lexie avoided agitating his memory by saying, "No apology is necessary, sir," and immediately began tuning the violin.

At the first sweep of the bow, which she handled with charming grace and art, Mr. Mims looked at his wife with a beaming smile and glittering eye. He was a lover of nature, communed with the music of the spheres and had a heart for joy. He once said he could hear music in the fall of a snow flake. Melodies suited his taste; he loved his home; his heart was Southern and Southern hearts are freighted with impulse and emotion.

"Home, Sweet Home," sobbed from the old violin, the darkies hurried into the dining-room, and, softly pulling the door ajar, listened; Aunt Bina covertly averted her face to the wall; the wife softly sighed; Sam Mims was melted; that noble melody reached his heart, as it does all true hearts, wherever heard in the wide world. The Swanee River was expressed with great power and beauty. No one since has been able to play it as she could. Under her touch it was a revelation of the heart's emotions. She then played the best tune of the first singer on the violin that ever appeared, and, closing, struck the major chord of that great song, which, in his early days, for love's sake, the great tone poet wrote.

She had spoken with her bow directly to the soul of Sam Mims and kindled emotions too tender to disturb. She quietly put the old violin in its case, and, by that common movement which takes place without previous arrangement between persons affected by refined emotions or deep distress, they silently retired for the night.

Next morning Sam Mims asked which way they were bound, and, upon being told, directed a double team of blooded bays to be hitched to the new spring wagon covered with shining black canvas, and, refusing to listen to any declining, sent them to Roan in charge of his son.

To the latter he said, "My son allow them to pay no bills. Secretly pay those with whom you stay and pretend they charged nothing. Do all you can to make them comfortable, for I am satisfied this morning that she is the same girl who so bravely came to our house and got me to furnish a horse to that fine looking wounded soldier to get away on. You remember that soldier."

"Yes, father, his name was Robert Hope."

"That's it. I got a letter from him yesterday saying he was back from Canada by way of Boston and would come to see me during the summer. Now, be careful with these people, they are certainly in great distress, and there is a mystery about them which it would be impolite to pry into."

They were off. In that sweet month of May they traveled the same route Sill's division took to Frankfort in October, '62, and on which he was moving the day the heroic battle of Perryville was fought. On the way to Roan the talk was light and commonplace. When the road was shady, Lexie played at intervals upon the old violin to while away the tedium of the trip. Tom Mims was surprised at her increasing beauty, which grew on closer acquaintance. At first her features appeared a bit too large, because she wore her hair closely plaited or smoothly clinging to her head. But when she unloosed her hair and it floated freely about her shapely shoulders and the May breezes whispered through it, Sir Joshua Reynolds himself would have been delighted at the privilege of perpetuating her beauty.

When she played the violin Tom noted the rosy flush in her long, tapering fingers. Though her finely formed hand was browned—it was the hand Joel Hart used as a model in chiseling the wrist and hand which lay on the speaker's desk when the Legislature ordered the ashes of her dead sculptor from sunny Italy back to his native State. Those ashes now rest near the grave of Sunny Withers in the shadow of the battle monument. Lexie never posed for the altogether, yet she had a finer form than Ada Rehan, who posed for the silver statue that everybody in the universe saw at the World's Fair. Her chin had the smallest cleft in it permissible, but when she laughed it got larger and so beautiful that Tom seemed to try to take it away from her with his eyes.

Before he left them at the log tavern in which "Colonel" Patter laid off the battlefield of Bull Run and began recruiting for "Dixie," Tom took Ned aside, and, swearing him to secrecy, gave him a twenty-dollar gold piece and said, "If ever your young mistress needs this, give it to her and tell her you found it."

Ned promised and Tom drove away at such a furious pace that people stared at him and the pretty bays as he passed.

"Her eyes had the longest, silkiest lashes you ever saw," said he to his mother after his return, "and she got prettier every day. Her modest reserve and heaven-born music made me almost crazy to ask all about her. I had the most morbid feeling to know her that ever came over any one."

"My son, I am thinking you are in love," said his mother.

"If I am I don't know it, but if I always feel like I do now about her I am certain I'll never be happy unless I learn her history. She was so interesting," said he in his frank, boyish way.

XXIX.

THE next morning the tavern keeper was confidentially courteous to his new guests.

"Where are you from?" inquired the host of "The War Tavern," the name given it the day after Lee surrendered. He addressed himself to Aunt Bina, who was wholly incompetent to cope with his long experience in extracting from strangers their private affairs.

Aunt Bina responded, "We are from Louisville."

"You must have pressin' business to bring you so fur in such a busy season of the year," said he.

Aunt Bina knew not what to say. Lexie answered, "Yes, we are looking after some business matters here in which we are told we have an interest."

"What kind of business is it?" was his next question.

"I can not tell you correctly," said she, "until I see Mr. Wolf."

He was so anxious to find out all about them that he tendered his services at once to go with Lexie Hallen to see 'Squire Wolf. She accepted the officious offer, and, leaving Aunt Bina at "The War Tavern," went with him, Ned trailing along after fearing something might happen to Miss Lexie. They found Fate

Wolf at his pension office in the Hallen house. The tavern-keeper essayed to introduce her, but Fate Wolf, breaking through all precaution, cried, "Howdy, hunney! I'm turrible glad to see ye! en so'll Scatlett be when she sees ye."

The tavern-keeper looked insistent, even amazed, but Fate Wolf, his cunning reasserting itself, said to him, "This little gyrl lives down yander whur we us'd to market part of our subter-shoots, en I got powerful well 'quainted with her'n her folks. Now ef ye'll go back to the tavern I'll take up her case right now."

This threw the keeper of "The War Tavern" clear off the trail of his curiosity. Thinking it was a pension case, he said, "When you git her papers fixed, bring her over to dinner and eat a bite yourself."

Turning, he left the room.

Fate Wolf told her all he could, then took her to the County Clerk and introduced her, saying, "This little gyrl wants to know somethin' soever you mout know, but yit I can't tell her," and withdrew, having told Lexie to "say nothin' to nobody" about him or what he was doing for her.

She saw the delicacy of his position and appreciated his assertion that "I alays likes to see wimmin righted en pertected."

The Clerk did not like Penn Grabbé, and, as soon as she told him that she was the only child of Richard Hallen, he said, "I know all about it. The tax sale was irregular. No notice, no advertisement of the sale, and it confers no title on Penn Grabbé, but you will have to pay him four dollars and eighty cents, the interest and fifty per cent. for the privilege of redemption."

"But," said she, "I have not got that much money."

"I will lend it to you," said the Clerk, "and you can pay me back out of the rent he owes you."

"That is very kind of you, sir," said she.

He then counted up the interest, cost and per centum to redeem the house and grounds.

He handed her the money, locked his office and started with her to "The War Tavern," but, seeing Penn Grabbé riding in from his canvass for Congress, said, "I had better go back; you can go by yourself to the tavern," and abruptly returned to his office.

Penn Grabbé uniformly went to his pension office in his Hallen house first before mixing with the people of Roan. On this occasion Fate Wolf was seriously glad to see him, and told him impressively of Lexie Hallen's presence at "The War Tavern" with Ned and her aunt and what she was after, but affected not to know the exact *status* of things.

"But I've larned," said he, "that Lexie Hallen is the livin' bein' air at law uv Richard Hallen. I know it to be a fac uv my own nollige, en sense ye left I've hearn that your title haint good to this yer house, en ef it haint, en ye try to keep it frum that little gyrl, it'll beat ye fur Congruss shore."

"If I find out," said Penn Grabbé, "that Lexie Hallen is entitled to this house, I will be the first man to say she shall have it on equitable terms."

Fate Wolf said, "We'd better go to the Clark's

office, fur they've bean there, en that dimocrat will tell 'em all about the title, ef it be defectious, en I've hearn it's too strong in the nose uv the law."

By the time they reached the Clerk's office, Penn Grabbé had several workable schemes for the future mapped out in his strategic brain.

He took the Clerk aside, but found him cold and intractable. Seeing that nothing could be expected from that quarter, he immediately called on Lexie Hallen and her aunt. He said, "Miss Lexie, I am more than glad to see you, and Miss Hallen, your presence makes this a double pleasure."

Thanking him for his icy glee over seeing them, they relapsed into silence. It was a little embarrassing, but Penn Grabbé was not the man to be blocked by embarrassment or the delicacies of life, so he renewed the interview by saying, "When did you leave Louisville? How is Miss Julia?"

"She is dead," quiveringly responded Lexie.

"O, I am sorry of that, indeed I am," said he.

Silence again settled over the conversation. The Clerk walked in without ceremony, as was the custom of most persons who frequented "The War Tavern." He at once whirled his mental hammer at the nail head of the situation and struck it squarely.

"Mr. Grabbé," said he, "you are wrongfully in possession of this young woman's house and ground, and owe her back rent for nearly nine years."

"Sir," rejoined Grabbé, "I was just coming to that subject when you interrupted us. I shall take great pleasure in giving an account of my stewardship of the Hallen house if you will retire and allow so delicate a subject to be discussed by the parties interested."

"I'll retire, sir," said the Clerk, "but this thing's got to be done to a finish or I'll *take* an interest in it."

Being a candidate for Congress, Grabbé had his best manners to the front and amicably said to the Clerk, "As soon as she and I talk it over, we will gladly call you in to see that everything is done precisely right—there is no man I had rather trust."

"Thank you," said the Clerk, who walked out, feeling that one cubit had been added to his height by this consummate manager of ordinary men; this schemer on the ground floor of humanity; this counterfeit Tallyrand.

"Now, Miss Lexie, I will speak of the business referred to by the Clerk for fear we may be interrupted again by some intruder. You know I have been the friend of your family through thick and thin, and that my pocket is two thousand dollars lighter by getting your sentence changed. You may yet trust to my generosity and faithfulness. The rent is worth a good deal, say fifty dollars per year for nine years, and I have improved the property at a cost of more than the rent. You or your aunt, your other aunt being dead and unable to pay anything, owe me two thousand dollars by note. I need not go further to show the sacrifice I am about to make. Then, in short, you may redeem by paying the tax, interest and per centum, and I will give you half the rent and all the note for one moiety of the property."

Lexie and Aunt Bina being moneyless women, uninformed as to the value of the house and grounds, and fearful that the note and its history might become public, and also anxious to relieve themselves from its overhanging power, agreed to the terms. The Clerk was called in, the terms were explained to him and he said at once that two thousand dollars was not a sacrificing price for one-half, counting the improvements at only two hundred and twenty-five dollars, but said the rent was rather low.

Lexie said, "We have given our word to the terms and prefer not to break it."

The house was redeemed. Penn Grabbé paid Lexie two hundred and twenty-five dollars and handed to Aunt Bina the note, which was based on no consideration, but extortion, made possible by Jerry Burr's brutal reign over the fair soil of the first daughter of the Union. It is said, while he ruled, robbed and massacred her people, the sun never shone bright in the old Kentucky homes, but rose in clouds and sank in smoke and fire. The dawn of peace, however, swept away the clouds and the descending sun of righteousness set the western horizon in a blaze of glory, and Jerry Burr, gnashing his teeth, disappeared in the gloom of his own dark conscience never to return again.

The Clerk prepared cross-deeds and Penn Grabbé signed one and Lexie Hallen started to sign the other when a question arose as to her age. She was in her nineteenth year. Penn Grabbé promptly interposed, saying, "I know Miss Lexie and her word is as good as her bond. I am willing to take her deed, for she will ratify it when she becomes of age."

"I certainly will," said she.

Both deeds were duly acknowledged and recorded. Thus Penn Grabbé and Lexie Hallen became joint tenants of her father's house. He insisted that she and her aunt should at once take possession, except of the office reserved for himself and Fate Wolf. This was done. With Ned's assistance, Lexie and Aunt Bina soon had the premises in order and by an outlay of a few dollars they went to housekeeping with lighter hearts than had beat in their bosoms since the war closed.

The season for gardening had begun and Lexie improvised a sun bonnet, Ned borrowed a hoe and a shovel from the keeper of "The War Tavern" and Aunt Bina filled her apron with garden seeds, and they all sallied forth into the balmy air, into the sunshine and liberty of labor to exercise the great geoponic art. They meant to make a living by the sweat of the face and be happy in toil, as toiling millions are.

Up rode "Colonel" Patter and talked to them while Long-Leaper poked his nose over the fence and nipped at the red rosebuds. This was surprising. The "Colonel" had on good clothes. His hat was a big new felt and he appeared more like the *ante bellum* orator than he had since the Fourth of July, 1861. He seemed to be genial, was rather pale and acted as if possessed of a burden which he wanted to unload. He begged a word with the young lady whom he recognized directly he reached the fence.

"Well, what is it?" said she, not recognizing him.

"Madam, I heard you were here, and, knowing some of the dangers to life and honor in this region, I concluded to warn you to be careful, bar your doors of nights and send for me if you get in trouble."

He immediately rose to a heroic position and quickly rode away, giving her no time to recover from the immensity of the surprise. This was dramatic, as "Colonel" Patter always liked to be, but, before he was out of sight, she called him to mind and regretted her apparent indifference.

Every day Penn Grabbé interested himself in their welfare, until his visits and advice became tiresome. She remembered his actions in taking her to Fate Wolf's home in the jaws of adamant, but credulously thought it might have been intended for the best, as Fate and Mrs. Wolf showed no signs of being in conspiracy with him, and now that circumstances had brought them into daily contact, she determined to dispel all suspicions and treat Penn Grabbé kindly for gratitude's sake, believing, as she did, that he had saved her from the Dry Tortugas at great risk and expense.

His race for Congress was growing warm, and whenever he was not out canvassing he was explaining to Lexie that he would be elected, had been her friend, was rich for the region and she ought to marry him as a matter of principle. In fact, he said she owed that much to him. His love was of the mind and of the passions, but not of the heart, so he urged his suit from the standpoint that all are governed by interests, by treasures which moth doth corrupt and thieves break through and steal. He knew that some are moved by the oppression of an obligation to discharge it. But to all of his overtures she firmly said no, at the same time expressing her gratitude for his past friendly acts in her behalf. Finally he came to believe that she was grateful enough to submit to be his wife if he could get her into his power and compromise her honor if she refused. The thought was at once materialized by his brain into a scheme, but election demands averted his attention for a time and pension frauds were hinted at by his opponents in such manner as required his pension performances to be looked after and guarded immediately. Fate Wolf had kept an eye on his maneuvers and made it a point to go into the family room, which was across the hall from his office, and talk to Aunt Bina and Lexie every day.

In these conversations he disclosed more doubt of Penn Grabbé than he was aware of, and in his constant reference to the law of pensions let drop many a remark that might have led to unpleasant discoveries had the listeners been detectives. As it was, he passed with them for an uneducated sage in that particular law. He gathered some scraps of fact and knowledge between times that laid the foundation for future guessing and doubting and hedging on his part when Grabbé got too mysterious to suit him.

The Hallens planted and cultivated their garden like experienced horticulturists, and its beauty in midsummer was remarked by all the town which had at one time or another been attracted to the house by Lexie's exquisite violin playing. Everybody that came in would ask her to play. People of Roan never ceased begging her to play, and she seemed never to tire of pleasing them. They usually listened in stolid earnestness, complimenting the performance with strong but unwordy exclamations. Soon she became the favorite of everybody.

Penn Grabbé was beaten for Congress by the Honorable Pat Riot, who could excel him in anecdotes, platitudes and pension promises. Thenceforward Penn Grabbé gave up office seeking and devoted himself to pension practice and to the one supreme passion of his mind and flesh.

XXX.

THE morning after all the returns for Congress were in, and no hope for Penn Grabbé's election remained, he sat at his office table talking to Fate Wolf, who was standing in the middle of the floor listening. The latter was cunningly amazed at Grabbé's veiled suggestions.

"Whatsumever do ye want me to do with the little gyrl, ef I hides her at the Rocky Gorge?"

"Why, 'Squire, I'd like for you to keep her there until I marry her. She is willing, but does not want to say so, because her aunt is so opposed to me."

"Must I ax her ef she art willin'?"

"No, no, not for a patriot's pension, for she would say no, and the fun of carrying her off in the night would be spoiled. You must not disarrange our plans, and I'll give you a thousand dollars in gold the day after the marriage and take you in as a full pension partner."

Fate Wolf's cupidity rose in the plentitude of its power and for the time being slew the good purposes which always began to form themselves out of his better impulses when woman's honor appeared to be in jeopardy. He wanted the money; he wanted the notoriety of the partnership; he wanted half of the pension profits, which had begun to be enormous to men like he, but fear of injuring Lexie and treachery on the part of Grabbé held his consent in abeyance, but only for a short time—then he agreed with the stronger will, supported as it was by the root of all evil.

Before the complicated scheme could be filtered into Fate Wolf's cunning but cumbersome intellect, Lyt Wardrip, who was teaching school at the mouth of Tippling Fork, dropped in to employ Penn Grabbé to obtain a pension for him. The three at once entered into a discussion of the subject of pensions.

Wardrip said, "The farmers who pay taxes are the stingiest taxpayers in the nation."

"I believe they are," said Grabbé.

"Yes," said Wardrip, "they're always grumbling about taxes for pensions. They forget that the Union soldiers won the war and saved every bit of property North from confiscation by the rebels. By rights our soldiers are entitled to at least one-half of all the farms, well stocked at that, north of Mason and Dixon's line."

"Howmuchsomever air they uv rights to south uv that thair line?"

"All of everything," promptly responded Wardrip to Wolf.

"The people air turrible tired uv taxes, en ef anuther way to git pensions outen uv 'em wuz blazed out it would be a site better fur the 'Publican party," said Wolf.

"But there is no other way," cried Wardrip, "and

they'll just have to stand it. Taxing the people is a slow, good, easy way of dividing the property North with our soldiers and their blood and married kin, who are nearer to them than hayseed taxpayers, merchants, bankers, bar-keepers and other dressy do-nothing classes of society. In course of time, by taxes heaped on a little more and more every year or two by Congress, a fair divide between the soldiers and the fat farmers can be made and the farmers won't feel it so mighty much. Why, what would two hundred million dollars a year be divided up amongst the long-tailed kin of the Union soldiers? Grant was talking through his hat when he said twenty-five million dollars a year would be enough! Then look at the soldiers who will get disabled by being sick a quarter of a century after the war, and some of them will get disabled by sickness if they live to be a hundred. It's true, not many, for the number we had in the field, were killed or wounded or disabled in battle, and there's not a very great many widows and orphans left by them. But would you let their blood kin suffer? or their wife's people work themselves to death? Now I don't, and most of the pensioners on Tippling Fork don't (and I think I can speak for the majority) want our half of this country collected in any one year."

"Go right on in your remarks, they are good and to the point," encouragingly said Grabbé.

"Well," said Wardrip, "there's another thing that's wrong in this free country. Congressmen from the farming districts are too strict in making pension laws. It's got so a man can hardly be honest and get a pension, although Congress intends everybody to have one. To get their rights, I am satisfied one-half, if not more, of the people on Tippling Fork, and it's over ninety miles long, have committed what I call white perjury for themselves or the pension attorneys who can't practice half their claims through without it."

"Thet's jist so to my own nollidge en 'sperience in takin' uv affidavys," blurted out Fate Wolf without due consideration.

Penn Grabbé bridled up and sought to divert the conversation. Wardrip said, "I want to say one more thing and I'll quit. If I had the power, I would make the taxpayers, for they have all the property, support every Union soldier until he dies, and feed and clothe his descendants, his wife's kin, and his blood kin to the third and fourth generations."

"Mr. Wardrip," said Grabbé, "you are the first broad-gauged patriot I have heard talk since the war."

"He soots me," said Fate Wolf.

"Now state the facts in your own case," cried Penn Grabbé dramatically. "I know they will be true, for truth and justice grow in the rarefied air of the mountain tops of pension patriotism, while stinginess and demagoguery flourish in the rich, fat soil of the dead-level plains of farming politics."

After this lofty speech, Wardrip, who had already gorged his moral nature with a great lie, allowed Grabbé to strike every tendency to truth left in him prostrate at the foot of the bad eminence of thrifty falsehood which Grabbé himself had raised upon his own sandy foundations for the wind and rain of life to beat against. It took the latter but a few moments to discover Wardrip was not as blind as he looked. The virus which had slightly shrivelled the first tunic of his eyes had spared the fine elastic membrane of the cornea, leaving its perfect transparency as God had made it, but it had made havoc of his eye-lashes, not one of which was left, and reddened the lids until Wardrip could plausibly play blind for a pension, were a miracle performed to make him see.

He claimed, in his declaration, that he, like old Gobbo in the Merchant of Venice, was sand blind, gravel blind from marching through the burning sands of Georgia, but the truth was that the virus which injured his eyes came from disease contracted long after the war was over.

Grabbé dated back Wardrip's blindness, and old Jo Soaks, who subsequently drew a dependent pension, made affidavit that it resulted from the effects of the sands of Georgia, which were blinding bright, during Sherman's march to the sea—from sun by day and incendiary fires by night. Jo Soaks refused to sign his affidavit until he added, "I don't believe thar's a sound-eyed man in Sherman's army left, en they ort to git pensions while they kin see, en not wait tell they git too blind to git up their pension papers."

Lyt Wardrip was promptly granted a pension, which, with arrears and increases to the present date, has yielded him twenty thousand, eight hundred and fifty-four dollars, yet he remains among the discontented!

Wardrip's success caused applications to increase amazingly, and for the whole of the ensuing year Grabbé had but little time to press his claims to the hand of Lexie. Cupidity was a greater passion than love with Grabbé, hence "business before pleasure" was his favorite motto. One day when pension complications were becoming uncontrollable and dangerous, he crossed the hall, determined to make his final appeal to Lexie for her hand. Fate Wolf sat at the affidavit table, as usual, and, while Grabbé was engaged in the forlorn effort to corrupt a pure heart and deceive an honest mind, Fate Hicks, of color, made his appearance and demanded a pension. This was the free negro boy whom "Fate" Wolf kidnaped before the war and was trying to sell as a slave in Lexington, when Colonel Jack May had him arrested and the boy released.

"Well, well, this beats ennything ever I seed," cried 'Squire Wolf. "Afore the war I warn't posted ag'in sellin' free niggers, but hev larned sense, en I'll make up fur that thar onjestice by gittin' you a pension; a onjestice what give me a stickin' nickname what sticks yit."

Fate Hicks stood stolid and speechless as he recognized this war abolitionist and heard the change of mind which had been wrought in him by the struggle for the Union.

"Whatsumever air yer grounds fur a pension?"

"Well," said Fate Hicks, "I wus took up fur a wag'ner en sarved two year, en quit in '63."

"That'll do," said 'Squire Wolf. "Wus ye injoored by the weather ur sculped by the rebels, ary one?"

"I got frost bit, but hit wur arfter the war."

"Never you mind days nur dates. I'll bet that thar frost fell endurin' uv the war, en Penn Grabbé kin git a pension on it ez easy ez slippin' eend foomust off a slick rock into the river when a feller is asleep a fishin'."

Penn Grabbé came in looking disconcerted, but immediately, and adroitly prepared the papers of Fate Hicks.

Before many moons 'Squire Wolf's prediction was fulfilled. The way this claim upon the bounty of Government came about was very natural. Fate Hicks, having drunk too much at a political speaking, was unable to get home, and from necessity slept in a fodder shock. The night was bitter cold, and the toes of his left foot, which got from under the fodder during the latter part of the night, were unfortunately frozen off. The sole cause of his drinking too much on that occasion resulted from over-excitement growing out of his support of the Government side of the debate. The legal effect of all these facts and the danger he had faced while battling for the Government were deftly jointed into his pension papers, consequently he is not a charge upon the people of Branch County. The Government being better able to support him than the people of that county, it is thought, by its best casuists, his pension was worthily bestowed, since it had many precedents in the practice of Penn Grabbé to support it.

Following the case of Fate Hicks, there was placed in Grabbé's hands another claim which required his best skill. At the battle of Richmond, previously described in this history, Dan Battle was slain. This fact appeared on the army rolls and his comrades reported that he was buried on the battlefield. His name, however, was mispelled on the rolls, for there it was plainly Bottle.

Grabbé discovered the error and at once sent for Dan Bottle, who lived on Tippling Fork, five miles below the mouth of Drinkard's Creek. This Dan Bottle had never been in the army, but, after staying about Grabbé's office several days and receiving instructions, he returned to his home and separated from his wife, Miranda, taking up his residence on Drinkard's Creek.

Thereafter he began to be called Danby Bottle and frequently told his neighbors that his twin brother, Dan Bottle, had been killed at Richmond, and that he had been compelled, from his notions of duty, to remain with his brother's widow and children to take care of them until the children got large enough to help their mother.

This story was believed, and Danby Bottle's disinterestedness was the talk of the creek from its mouth to its head.

In due season Grabbé sent for Miranda Bottle, and she signed and swore to a declaration for a pension as the widow of Dan Bottle, alias Dan Battle, killed in the battle of Richmond. The affidavits were precisely in accord with the army rolls, and Miranda Bottle received a pension without let, hindrance or hitch in the proceedings. Her six minor children were also placed on the pension rolls, and the family were afterwards spoken of by all the neighbors as "a mighty well-to-do family."

Danby Bottle was very attentive to the widow and orphans of his supposititious twin brother, visiting them almost daily and receiving from his neighbors Scriptural plaudits for his visits to the widow and the orphan, and for keeping himself unspotted from the world.

For a quarter of a century after the close of Penn Grabbé's usefulness, as shown in the following chapter, the widow regularly drew her pension, and on every Fourth of July made her children celebrate.

Many years had elapsed when a man calling himself Dan Battle, who was reported killed in the battle of Richmond, mysteriously appeared in the streets of Roan, and, after a few days, became, by accident, acquainted with the pension attorney who had succeeded to Penn Grabbé's practice and methods. After a brief consultation, the attorney announced the joyful news in Roan that the husband of the widow Miranda Bottle had turned up at last. A meeting was arranged to take place between them, and a number of citizen pensioners went along to witness the joyful reunion. The pension attorney went ahead, however, to break the news to her, which he did with professional caution.

When the party appeared she was agitated, but the moment she laid her eyes upon him, who had been given up as dead, she recognized her long lost husband and declared that she would cease to draw a pension as his widow, and the department was so notified.

He gave an excellent account of his absence and why he had roamed over the Northwest ever since the war closed, showing war wounds that he had received by accident in a saw mill. The widow vehemently supported his pretensions, but her eldest daughter repudiated him; the sobriquet, "Battle," he said, was won by his gallantry, and the war department made a note of it on the rolls. Our generous Government granted him a pension with back pay, amounting to nineteen thousand two hundred and eighty dollars. This sum was equally divided between them, and Dan Bottle, alias Battle, disappeared shortly, without rhyme or reason, never to return. The widow mourned for twelve months the waywardness of her husband and then applied for a divorce, which was granted on the statutory ground of abandonment for one year. The course of the Judge who granted the divorce was generally approved by the people on Tippling Fork.

During all these years and the happening of these multiplied events, Danby Bottle had dropped from public notice and was regarded by his immediate neighbors as a bachelor hermit, but, when Miranda Bottle lost her husband the second time he took a different view of his duty as a twin brother, and, in spite of the doctrine preached by the hardshell Baptist on Tippling Fork, he married his brother's widow and restored the *statu quo* which Uncle Sam still maintains.

XXXI.

WITH Lexie the summer, fall and winter had flown on leaden wings, for she had submitted from generosity for supposed favors to the most repulsive suit ever invented by a scheming mind. She was, indeed, unhappy, but fortunately her misery found expression in the music of her dear violin. She invoked the genius of harmony and it broke forth at last from misfortune and loneliness which so often give birth to the purest emotions and loftiest aspirations. She would often stroll away into the ivy-grown grottoes of the woods and play to the wild streams, whose gentle undertones accompanied her violin in a new song—a song of the winds and woods and waters. She climbed to the mountain tops and with the breezes in the pines blended the deep tones of her noble instrument. The echoes of the rocks gave back the sighs of her soft-breathing cremona, and nature, in unison with art, disclosed new harmonies not understood before in the history of music. She felt a new-born power, and, seeking to evoke its mystery, learned that the music of nature held mysteries and pathos yet undiscovered. She disclosed her secret to Aunt Bina and played with such spirit-flowing harmony that the latter's heart was filled with superstition at the phenomena. She had never before heard the music of the waters, the breezes and the echoes flow from the heart of the violin. Feminine art and masculine nature had produced a beautiful new birth of music and of song. New strains which seemed old and an old touch that was new were born of Lexie's misery, and, unfortunately for artists of the mystic power of sound, died with her life.

Old men and even outlaws, who yet live in Branch county, talk of her music with tears in their voices and tell how she stole it from the spirits of the hills, from the rocks and streams while wandering in "The woods of Roan."

Lexie's first year in Roan was pitilessly dreary. She was in constant fear from the heavy-booted claimants who noisily trod through the hall into Grabbé's pension office or came into her room to light their pipes or ask for a tune. Loud talk, intermingled with curses, often reached her ears, and "Colonel" Patter's warning kept her uneasy and alarmed at night. In his last interview, Lexie discovered Grabbé was an uneasy man and his so-called wooing more like a menace than anything else. When he left her she told her aunt of the change in his manner and stated she believed "Colonel" Patter's warning had reference to him. Their uneasiness that evening was painful, but it became torture when nightfall darkened the town.

A heavy mist filled the valley and the great fog-enveloped mountains to the eastward looked threateningly mysterious. The doors were barred and Ned lay on his pallet of fresh straw by the outer door with his axe near at hand. At midnight he dreamed the window was hoisting and glaring eyes from the dark outside were looking in upon him. He turned over, and, rising from his humble pillow, said, "Who's dar?" No answer came, and, falling back upon his bed, he went to sleep again. Once more the apparition of mischief haunted him. He dreamt that he went to Miss Lexie's room and found her dead. He sprang to his feet just as the bar to the door gave way from the heavy pressure of the heavy shoulders of three men who stood in black masks before him.

In an instant the axe was swung by Ned, with the courage of Richard Cœur de Lion, and one of the three fell backward from the door. Before he could recover the axe for another blow, the quick flash of a knife and a pistol ball struck his faithful bosom and he fell to the floor.

His blood gushed from his wounds and through his mouth; his convulsed lips could not cry out; he struggled for a moment; drew up his feet as if trying to rise, but a quiver of his poor frame followed and Ned was no more! His honest, brave heart had ceased to beat and he had gone, where? None of us know.

While Ned was struggling in his last agony, the kidnappers rushed against the door leading into Lexie's room and broke it from its hinges. Seizing her in their terrible grasp, they hurried into the hall.

There they quickly bandaged her mouth and eyes and dragged her toward the door while she struggled desperately against their progress.

In her frantic endeavors to release herself, her temple struck a sharp angle at the stairway which leads up from the hall to the half story above it, and she dropped almost lifeless to the floor. They gathered her in their strong arms and bore her to the outer door, her feet touching Ned's fallen body.

Citizens who had been aroused by the report of the pistol and the cries of Aunt Bina came running to their rescue and reached the entrance before the kidnappers could drag Lexie from the door to which she had caught as she revived from the shock received by the collision with the sharp angle of the stairway.

The kidnappers were forced to release her and fly through the darkness, pursued by the infuriated citizens. Lexie was carried to her room more dead than alive and Aunt Bina was picked up quite unable to speak.

The indignation of the people knew no bounds. Nearly every man and woman in Roan sat up the rest of the night, and as many as could watched the bedside of Lexie until morning. She was prostrated by the terrible fright and injuries she had received. She was in a precarious condition; her pulse was high; she had a burning fever and was very nervous. Since "Colonel" Patter's warning, a vague uncertainty of impending danger had hung over her like the sword of Damocles, and, when assailed by the kidnappers, her nerves gave way altogether. The injury on the temple was serious and her condition dangerous. An ungraduated doctor was called in, but, never having done anything but act on a pension board of examiners, did nothing, which was the best thing he could do.

Fate Wolf walked about the office, looked at Ned lying on the hall floor awaiting the Coroner's inquest, picked up everything he saw and said very little to any one.

Roan was excited as never before. A searching party started on the trail of blood which coursed in the direction of Tippling Fork. They met Grabbé coming to his office, as usual, and told him of the tragedy. He heard the details with perfect composure, manifesting so little interest in them that some of the Vigilants remarked upon his conduct.

He rode on to Roan, spent most of the day in his office and seemed to avoid conversation with every one whom the met.

Next morning the Vigilants returned, having lost all trace of the fugitives after reaching the rugged cliffs of Tippling Fork. They began talking about Grabbé's indifference.

"Colonel" Patter had heard the news and came to Roan and talked loudly against the perpetrators of the outrage. He kept away from Grabbé's office, which was unusual. Nothing else but the crime was talked of. Incessant insinuation, under the breath, went on against Grabbé, but no direct evidence could be found connecting him with it. Certain habitues of his office failed to appear during the week following Ned's murder, and a visit to their houses found them all at home save Eph Soaks. His wife made insufficient explanations of his absence and diligent search and inquiry failed to discover him.

In the course of the week the community began to settle down to the conviction that Grabbé had planned the abduction of Lexie which resulted in failure and the murder of Ned. Suspicion pointed its hundred fingers at him. Finally he was arrested and released on bail to stand his trial the next Monday.

Every able-bodied pensioner in that section, armed to the teeth, came to Roan. The news had reached the bluegrass and was published in the papers far and wide. Tom Mims read it and at once hurried to Roan, arriving there the Sunday before the day set for the trial. He called to see Lexie, but she was too ill to receive him.

The morning his trial was set Grabbé made a speech from the door in defense of which Ned had lost his life, and pointed, apparently with pity, to Ned's blood that stained the floor, saying, "Thank God, none of it is on these loyal hands," holding them high and dramatically above his head. The pensioners shouted and Lexie's nerves gave way. This condition was followed by great depression of mind and soon she became delirious.

Grabbé had tried to see her several times since Ned's murder, but the presence of neighbors and the excuse that she was too sick to see him kept him out. He made bold, however, to call just after his speech.

He was told she was out of her head, but went in notwithstanding and made a long story to Aunt Bina of what he had said and done, giving great prominence to his sorrow and suffering at being suspected of such a crime.

While he was talking Tom Mims called again, and this time he was admitted, for Grabbé's presence was a menace to Lexie's life. Tom Mims gave Grabbé a warning look and Grabbé left immediately. Then Tom spoke to Lexie, but her mind still wandered and she did not know him. She looked up into his face with a weak, pained look that touched a chord, which had hitherto been strung. He did not realize the force of that sad, painful look.

Lexie was becoming restless and Aunt Bina said, "You must rest now; Mr. Mims, you can call again."

Their eyes met as he rose to go. Her brief, bewildered gaze was tender and full of meaning, such as mixes up emotions, leaving the heart in delightful uncertainty.

Grabbé's trial was postponed for another week. He was using the law's delay to head off public sentiment that was setting in against him; but the delay was a mistake, for adverse public opinion gathered greater force and Tom Mims was enabled to communicate with Robert Hope and have him present to aid in the prosecution. The latter had studied law after his marriage and was rising into prominence.

During the summer following his marriage he had visited the Mims, and, in conversation about the war and their several experiences, learned of Tom that he was corresponding, in a formal way, with Lexie Hallen and that he was almost in love with her.

Robert Hope had, therefore, renewed his interest in her fate. When Tom's letter informing him of her dangerous condition, and urging him to come and aid in the prosecution of Grabbé, was received, he started for Roan, arriving there the morning the case was set for trial. His interest in the case centered around Lexie, whom he gratefully remembered for the part she and the murdered boy, Ned, had taken in his escape and flight from the prison hospital at Louisville. She was better on the day of his arrival, and he and Tom at once called to see her. The room was clean and tidy. Large red roses which had grown on the bushes "Colonel" Patter's horse had nipped hung from the lips of buckets and pitchers which were set in different places about the humble apartment.

Lexie's brown hair lay scattered about on a white pillow. Her head was propped up a little, and, when Robert Hope entered, her sad brown eyes lighted up with memory and gladness, and the cleft in her chin seemed to smile. Every expression of her fine face was a charming recollection and a token of the bitter past and of the fleeting joy of the short present. Tom had considerately informed her of Robert Hope's presence in order to avoid any excitement when he should come in.

The bed was drawn between the door and window to catch the breeze from the Cumberland Mountains that constantly swirled down on the Roan Valley in summer. Suffering had wrought lines of pain on the low, broad brow which so becomes a brown-haired woman. They sat down on either side of the bed, and Robert took her hand in his and began talking gently and cheerfully. Since his arrival Tom had not missed a day—not a morning, evening or night—in his visits to her, and had quite supplanted Aunt Bina and the quack doctor, who now only gave directions for Tom to carry out, if he liked them. Lexie said Tom was a fine nurse, and so he was, for he had learned of nursing that the best nurses are always in love with the patient.

Aunt Bina had grown ten years older in the last fortnight, and took but little notice of what was going on around her. She sat at the foot of the bed, where she could see Lexie's dear face and hear all she said.

Robert Hope said, just as if he were talking for fun, "Lexie, I believe you could ride to Sam Mims' now if the escape of a rebel were to be effected."

She faintly smiled at Hope's effort to encourage her, but languidly said, "Those days are gone now, and what is left of my life is but a span. The cruelties of war and the inhumanity of poverty no longer deter me as they once did, yet I sometimes think it good to be poor, if poverty did not so often give the wicked the opportunity to destroy the good and wrong the victory over right."

This nearly broke Tom's heart, and his emotion almost overcame him.

Before the conversation could start again, the Court House bell began to ring for the trial of Penn Grabbé, and, with kind, encouraging words, they bade her be quiet, saying they would return.

"Come as often as you can," said she, "for I will be glad to see you, and you can tell me what Tom has been telling me about."

"What is that?" inquired Robert Hope.

She smiled faintly and said, "You know. It is about your marriage with Lema Sayr, whom I love so well."

The bell continued to ring—it seemed to toll—and they left for the trial.

As they went along, Robert Hope said, "We must prepare for the worst. Poor Lexie is not long for this world. I must write to Mrs. Hope to come at once."

They entered the court-room, where "the grand human thing called law and the great divine thing called justice were visible."

The Justices of the Peace—one of whom could not read reading and one of whom could not write writing, but both of whom respected the majesty of the law, and when sworn had a superstitious awe for justice—occupied the Judge's seat.

Grabbé sat to the left, just behind his able counsel imported from the beautiful bluegrass region to defend him.

The public prosecutor occupied the right, with no client by his side, save the invisible State. Robert Hope entered and took his seat near the public prosecutor. The senior Justice called the case:

"The Commonwealth of Kentucky
against
Penn Grabbé.
He is charged with willful murder."

Grabbé and his lawyers put their heads together. The public prosecutor and Robert Hope passed a single word and announced "the State is ready."

"May it please the Court, the defendant is also ready," said Kentucky's famous criminal lawyer—Tech Flawhaven.

The witnesses on both sides were marshaled, sworn and separated, each side calling Fate Wolf and "Colonel" Patter.

The warrant was read and Penn Grabbé rose himself and pleaded in a calm, firm voice, "Not guilty."

By agreement, the statements made by Lexie Hallen before the Coroner's jury were detailed by the foreman of that informal, antiquated and somewhat useless body. In this Grabbé had great advantage, for she had made no allusion to his previous course with her.

After several citizens who frightened off the kidnappers the night Ned was murdered had testified, one of the Vigilants that had gone in pursuit next day was introduced. He was examined in chief by Robert Hope, as follows:

What is your name? Linton Lynch.

Were you with the Vigilants the next day after the murder of Ned Hallen? I was.

Did you see Penn Grabbé? I did.

Where? On the dividing ridge between this and Tippling Fork.

Was any conversation had with him? Yes.

What was it? Our leader told him of Ned's murder and what he knew about it.

What did Grabbé say? Nothing of importance. He expressed some surprise.

How did he look and act?

To this question counsel for the defense objected because the question called for the opinion of the witness. The Justices overruled the point.

The witness answered: His eyes were restless, his color changed a little, thought more than he spoke. He did not take much interest, and rode off.

Tech Flawhaven said he did not wish to cross-examine this witness.

Then "Colonel" Patter was called in and examined.

How long have you known the accused? Since the year A. D. 1855, when the Know Nothings were so bad.

Do you know of any deception he practiced on Lexie Hallen and her aunts just before the war closed? I have heard of that deception, but personally know nothing of it.

How did you hear of it? I first heard Fate Wolf tell of the outlay of two thousand dollars to save Lexie Hallen from the Dry Tortugas, but after the war I met Lieutenant Woorley, who had been on General Burr's staff, and he said it did not cost Penn Grabbé a cent, and Miss Hallen was not ordered out of the State, but unconditionally released.

Counsel for the accused objected to the answer because it detailed hearsay. The public prosecutor said, "We will make the evidence competent."

Robert Hope continued:

Did you communicate those facts to Penn Grabbé? I did.

What did he say? Nothing. He laughed.

Did you give Lexie Hallen any warning at any time? I did.

When? Last spring.

What was that warning? I gave no names, but I told her to keep her doors barred.

Why did you tell her to do that? Because I inferred —

Here an objection was interposed and sustained.

Cross-examined by Tech Flawhaven.

Are you the same "Colonel" Patter who deserted from the rebel army? I am not. I am the same *man* who escaped from their infuriated envy. I never joined their army.

Did Mr. Grabbé take you in and care for you on your return home? Well, yes, he took me *in* and used me. I never thought he cared for me much.

For what did he use you? I never knew exactly; but in a subordinate position connected in a remote way with his recruiting and trading.

Has he loaned you money? He has, but I paid it back.

Have you given him affidavits proving his accounts to be just against the Government? I have, in certain cases.

Have you any ill feeling toward the accused? I most certainly have, sir.

On what is it based? His mistreatment of Lexie Hallen.

Do you know, of your own knowledge, he mistreated her? I do not, but I have heard —

"I object to what you have heard," said Flawhaven, "I only want what you do know."

The cross-examination closed. The witness was directed to retire.

Fate Wolf was then called. The audience exhibited great interest as he took the stand and all eyes were riveted upon his face. He had refused to confer with the State's lawyers and great doubt existed as to how he would testify.

Direct examination by Robert Hope.

How long have you known the accused? Ever sense he got to be high shuruff en went to the Legislatur.

When was that? In '57 en '59.

How well have you known him since? Mitynigh es well ez a nigger use to know his master.

Have you had any business with him? I hev. Lots.

What sort? Well, fust and fomust we traded in hogs, mules, cattle, rekroots en subter-shoots. Arter the war we went into the pension trade en we air still a officerin together ontell this trouble cum up.

Do you know Lexie Hallen? Yes sir-ee, I do.

Did you know Ned Hallen, who was killed? I wus a quainted with him.

Where were you the night of his murder? I wus in my cabin in the Rocky Gorge.

When did you hear of his death? The follerin evenin'. Eph Soaks cum to my cabin wi' his sholder split open en sed that nigger Ned hed got killed. I axed him howsumever it wur dun en he sed he didn't know onless Penn Grabbé hed shot him to keep him from killin' two men en —

Tech Flawhaven shouted his objections and the hearsay was ruled out, but Grabbé's face turned deathly pale. Everybody was watching him and the Vigilants, who were attending the trial in force almost as large as the pensioners, showed signs of excitement. Order was restored and the evidence proceeded.

Tech Flawhaven:

Why didn't you tell these things as soon as you came to Roan after the killin? Howsumever do ye know but what I did?

Flawhaven told Hope to finish with the witness and he would cross-examine him then.

Robert Hope:

If you know, state the facts about the accused bringing Lexie Hallen to your house the year the war closed? Du ye want me to tell it all in my own way? Yes.

Well, he fotch her thar jist about two weeks afore Gineril Lee give up, en told me that Gineril Sherman had ordered wimmin a rested en Gineril Burr had exhyled Lexie. Scatlett tuck her in en fell in love with her en I got sot that a way myself. She's the nicest gyrl ever ye seed en kin beat a angel a playin' on his own harp. Penn Grabbé told me thet he paid two thousand to git her off en I believed him, yit he acted a leatle quare en I sed, Scatlett less watch him, en we did en wouldn't let him bother her nuther. Scatlett wanted to sick the dogs on him, yit I got her not to do it. Arter Ned cum en Lee give up I went off to Grabbé's en Lexie left fur home in the night. I hated that fur I had bean at hur house in Luisvil en they hed entreated me turrible nice. I've hearn sense thet he didn't pay no two thousand.

"Never mind what you heard," said Flawhaven.

Hope:

How came Lexie Hallen to come to Roan? I writ her a letter is what fotch her.

What did you write about? The Hallen house what belonged to her.

After she arrived, what was done about the Hallen house? Penn Grabbé give it up, yit he charged fur that two thousand he didn't pay en got half the house fur it.

How did the accused behave toward Lexie Hallen after she and her aunt moved into the house? He crossed the hall most ever' day en tried to cort Lexie, yit she wouldn't hev nuthin' to do with him 'cept listen en look trubbled.

Did he ever speak to you about hiding her at your house? One day, the day arter it wur knowed he wur beat fur Congruss, he axed me to keep her in the Rocky Gorge, nur to tell her aunt, fur that would spile the fun uv stealin' uv her off in the night.

Where did this occur?- In our pension offis.

Did you come to the office the morning after Ned was killed? I did.

What did you find? I found Ned dead, thet little gyrl purty nigh dead, en a empty catridge wur outside the winder at the front eend uv the hall en a hole shot through the winder what would a hit Ned ez he swang the axe back to kill two men, ez Eph Soaks told me he did, fur which he tho't Penn Grabbé shot him.

Tech Flawhaven complained to the Court because the witness stated hearsay before he could object. This point was not passed on.

Have you that cartridge? I hev.

Will you produce it? Yes, sir.

Here Fate Wolf produced the shell of an exploded pistol cartridge. Great curiosity to see it was shown all over the crowded house.

By this time the excitement in the audience was intense. Grabbé was pale and restless, the Justices uneasy; and signs of release on the part of the pensioners were manifest. The Justices consulted a moment and ordered the high Sheriff to summon four deputies and take the accused into custody pending the remainder of the trial.

This being done, Robert Hope proceeded with the examination.

'Squire Wolf, did you ever fit that cartridge shell in any pistol?

Penn Grabbé looked beseechingly at Fate Wolf and shook his head smilingly as he sat pale and nervous under the pitiless honesty of the witness.

It would be a onjestice to a little gyrl ef I wus to per-varry-kate en I hev to swear, fur I'm on oath in a cort uv jestice, thet I did fit it in a pistol.

Who's pistol was it? My ole fren's.

Whom do you mean, name the man? It wur Penn Grabbé's—and Fate Wolf shed tears, sincere, honest, repentant—and added, I agreed fur to keep the poor little gyrl ag'in ef she wur willin' to be stole, ez Grabbé told me she wur, en hit wur her aunt what wus objectin'.

The audience was amazed, the Vigilants were boiling with wrath, the pensioners were surprised at the disclosures and the prisoner seemed about to be enveloped in a tempest of destruction.

Flawhaven saw that it were worse than madness to try to stem the tide and at once arose and waived further examination, saying, "My client will trust to a future day when passion subsides and justice may have a chance to prevail."

The prisoner was committed to jail without bail. The Sheriff and guards, followed by the crowd, led him out of the court room and across the open court yard to the jail steps, which ascended on the outside of the building to the main entrance ten feet above the ground. At the door a square platform, four by six feet, received the top of the ladder-like steps. The sheriff, deputies and prisoner stopped on the crowded platform while the door was unlocking in full view of the people.

Penn Grabbé asked the privilege of saying a word in his own behalf, which was granted. By the time he had said, "My fellow citizens, I can explain away the evidence brought against me," his pension clients had occupied all the space about the foot of the steps and beneath the platform.

In an instant he saw his opportunity and sprang from the platform into their midst, and fled in the confusion to the nearest horse hitched to the Court House fence, and before the Sheriff and deputies recovered from their surprise and pushed their way through the crowd of pensioners, who were obstructing their movements, Penn Grabbé was gone. He soon reached the woods of Roan and easily evaded pursuit.

The Sheriff, deputies and angered Vigilants furiously followed him, but to no purpose. They soon returned, and a battle between them and the pensioners, who could not conceal their delight at Grabbé's escape, was narrowly averted.

Robert Hope and Tom Mims went immediately to see Lexie to quiet her in the event she should hear of the great excitement and imminent danger of bloodshed.

That night the pensioners howled about the streets, breathing out threatenings and slaughter against "Colonel" Patter, but were quite careful to say nothing inimical to Fate Wolf, for he knew too much about "affidavys" and facts on which their peace, plenty and pensions rested. He could pull down the whole fabric, though blind and bound to the pillars of the system which Grabbé had erected; and he could do it, living or dead, for he had the example of poor Ned, whose death had brought to a close a patriot's strategy.

XXXII.

IN the early dawn Roan was being deserted. The pensioners were riding away from its outskirts; the Vigilants were retiring to their homes.

The sun was rising over the highest eastern range of the Cumberlands, its rays were scattering the mists of the valley while the deep dark rents which opened the huge sides of these mountains were being penetrated, even to their wildest recesses, by the light. Ten thousand trees arching their trunks stood like myriad columns under a vast green canopy. Lock Ege's bald head glinted beneath the gilding rays when Lexie opened her languid eyes from a long night's sleep, during which her poor sickness-broken body had rested as though she were dead.

Tom Mims, who had fanned her while she slept during the earlier part of the night, stood by the bedside with dejected countenance, quivering lip and open hands ready for the wringing when her soft gaze sought his face and her low, tranquil voice said, "Good morning, Tom."

Agony unspeakable filled his plaintive response, and his hands rose and fell in love and grief.

The roses in the garden were exchanging dews for sunbeams, absorbing the blue and yellow rays while blushing blood red under the sun's early glances.

She said, "Open wide the door and let me look at the leaves and flowers."

Aunt Bina gently raised the latch and the sweet summer air left the red roses to fan the smooth forehead and the composed body which lay so calm and still.

Her hands were lying on the pink coverlet, open as if ready to take hold of the Saviour should he call. They were charming hands, for they could catch a sympathy as a bruised heart or the eyes of sorrow. Her lips were shut lightly, and the gentle upper curves of the corners seemed to smile, nay, a smile did hover there as she repeated the lines:

> "If I may trust the flattery of sleep,
> My dreams presage some joyful news at hand."

Robert Hope heard her as he entered, and said, "I bring you the joyful news; Lema is here."

A moment more and Lema lifted the chiselled hands about her neck and gently kissed Lexie's forehead, while saying those words which she alone could say to the suffering.

"You must get well; I can nurse you back to health and strength."

Robert and Tom were looking on with emotion. Robert unseen by Lexie slowly and sadly shook his head. Tom looked alarmed, but either could not or feared to move a muscle.

A few words were spoken to Aunt Bina and Lema sent Tom to the tavern for her satchel in which she had brought the silver cup and flask of war-time service and many medicines. It had almost everything in it that might do Lexie good.

While Tom was gone she said, "I am glad you are so tranquil, dear, for it will aid you to recover speedily."

"Ah," said Robert in a whisper to Lema as she mixed the medicines, "the Clerk of Heaven has issued the summons and the return will be brief."

Lexie drank a little of the wine poured from the silver flask and her eyes seemed filled with a brighter light. She gazed about the room and into the garden with a wistful, eager look, "This morning reminds me of my early life at the old home. I can see the big spring into which poor Ned fell, and feel the flutter of fear as I held him up with my little hands until father answered our screams and lifted him out half strangled. How I loved to 'run about the braes and pull the gowan fine,' and how I loved for my cheerful father to swing me, exultant, high into the air in the old swing hanging from the spreading elm that stood by the garden gate. I remember how he would lay aside his books and pen and sometimes spend the whole afternoon with Ned and me roaming about the great bluegrass fields and wide wood pastures, picking flowers and watching the birds and squirrels, while his cattle grazed on the distant hills. It is sweet to recall those early days, and my memory has hoarded them, and now they bear me golden interest."

"Well, well," said Lema, "the beginning of our lives often casts sunbeams upon the far-off close, making the approach to heaven all hope and relief."

"Yes, a blessed relief to those that weary-laden mourn," interposed Lexie.

"Dear, dear, but you will get well, my sweet one," said Lema, "be quiet now and I will watch you to sleep."

"I am quiet, but I can not sleep, for I want to talk to you to-day. It is going to be my last on earth and I want it all with you."

Her tones were so tranquil and sweet that Lema's eyes filled with tears. Looking in fear and pity at Lexie's snowy hands lying still, but hopefully open, she sighed, deeply thinking how beautiful they were —those curves and delicate lines, the hidden charms and graces that nestled in the hollows of those sweet hands, their secrets of charity and generous deeds treasured up and read by Him alone who never turned away a woman.

The hand is a mystery. It is divine. Its perfect fitness for the delicate uses of life is as pervasive as the demands of labor. Deft, subtle, strong and suited to the doing of all things, it has formed each part of every discovery and invention, and by its tracery preserved the thought of every brain. It is the medium, more delicate than the eye, of the passions. Its pathos goes straight to the heart. It speaks through the touch and the veins flow faster. Who has not felt the lover's glowing touch or the warm grasp of a friend? It is the instrument of God to fashion nature to man's use.

"I know what you are thinking," said Lexie, "I felt

my fingers on the strings of my old violin as plainly as if it were now in my hands. I heard its music so soft and sweet, my arm could feel the thrill of the bow across the strings. Now put your hand in mine and I will know what your heart feels."

Lema's heart rose in her bosom and great love filled her soul as she moved away in order to turn the current of sympathy which was running too high for Lexie's strength. Imperceptibly that strength was going. She waited until Lema again sat down beside her and then said calmly, "Now, tell me everything about you and Robert Hope."

Lema began the story, telling her all that happened to either of them from Shiloh to their wedding day. When she told Lexie that she had recognized Robert in that memorable duel, Lexie said, "I had a vague feeling then that you knew him. Go on now and tell me the rest."

"I will finish it after a while," said Lema, "I must not tell you too much at once, it will tire you."

At intervals during the day Lema told her the rest of her story, and late in the afternoon as the sun was sending his last rays into the little garden Lexie began where she had left off in the morning to tell the story of her trouble and her poverty and the trials of her short life. Lema Sayr, Robert Hope and Tom Mims, who had been joined by Fate Wolf, good old Scatlett and "Colonel" Patter, were the listeners. With tenderness and pain they listened quietly. Every feeling of their hearts was enlisted and burnt Lexie's words upon their minds forever. She talked on until the shadows began to fill the valley and, as day merged into night, dropped into soft slumber. Lema told Tom to go to the tavern and get a good night's rest, that the others in turn would sit up with Lexie.

He went to the tavern and was given the same room in which "Colonel" Patter clipped the big name from the Gazette and pasted it on the Enquirer to remove Fate Wolf's objections to volunteering for the South.

He layed him down, and from exhaustion soon fell into a light sleep. There was a low barometer prevailing and toward midnight he slept soundly under the sweet refrain the rain played upon the shingles, and as the thunder began to roll over the valley his dream grew wonderfully beautiful.

He dreamed that the end of the world had been predicted for a day near at hand, but that he refused to believe it, saying "it was superstition." He wavered a little, however, as even the strongest will. The sun hung high in the heavens when the day began to darken. First the sun grew dim. The air was still. Sounds grew ominous and it grew darker. The people gathered together. In the afternoon the sun began to throw off great pieces of light, flashing with intolerable radiance. The air grew denser and darker and awful in its stillness. The sides of the mountains were laid bare of tree and rock by the lightning. The whole valley was darkness and dawn, shadow and light, flashes and sheets of flame. The heavens were thickly sown with stars that glinted through the contending light and darkness. A shapeless shadow fell from the light of the stars and seemed to brood over the warring elements. Poising on slowly evolving wings, it began to take form until it came to view, a perfect woman with sky-blue eyes gently glancing mercy in every direction and at every one. Tom's dream had awed him into fear, but when the angel took his hand his fear left him. He felt guilty but not afraid, and said to the angel, "Have I been wicked and shall I be saved?" The angel laughed and said, "You shall be saved by your faults." The angel left him and hovered over Lexie and gazed into the lusterless eyes and calm white face.

He awoke to hear the rain pouring on the roof and some one knocking, knocking, knocking. He opened the door and Fate Wolf, wet and pale, said, "They wants ye to cum."

He hastily dressed and questionless trudged through the storm with a great weight at his heart. When they reached the house they went softly in. Tom approached the bedside.

Lexie's death was the result of depression of heart more than from the injury she received at the hands of Penn Grabbé's minions. From early girlhood sorrow had filled her breast. Her heart seldom beat in cheerfulness, though her spirit made many bright struggles to be free. But alas! it, too, finally shrank from the bitter touch of the world, and when the shock of alarm and the injury upon her dear temple were superadded to her burdened spirit, she fell beneath the combined weight and her gentle soul left its mortal tenement and passed beyond the morn.

They buried her in the garden under the rose bushes to await the call of Him who said blessed are they that mourn, for they shall be comforted. Was the cause of her life lost like the cause of her dear South? Did she too go down in gloom to rise in glory?

Good reader, you may now take your way and I shall take mine. May you love much, work hard, live cheerfully and die in peace.

www.ingramcontent.com/pod-product-compliance
Lightning Source LLC
Chambersburg PA
CBHW032058220426
43664CB00008B/1051